WANDERINGS
ON WRITING

WANDERINGS ON WRITING

Hi
Carmen,
Follow
you
dreams!

Essays by

JANE LINDSKOLD

Jane Lindskold

Table of Contents

To Paul and Bobbi – because you kept suggesting this book

To Jim – for walking with me every step along the way

Introduction: Forging the Golden Key

This is not a "how to write" book – or maybe I should say, it's not *only* a "how to write" book. It's also a window into how one writer has managed to deal with the complexities of both creating fiction and being a professional author.

Although I've been a full-time writer since mid-1994, when I chucked a reliable job as an assistant professor of English to move to New Mexico, there was a time when I had to juggle both fiction writing and a demanding job. Some of the tricks I learned then have served me well throughout my career. I'll share those tricks, some of which I adapted from what I heard other writers say they did. Hopefully, you'll be able to adapt some of these for yourself.

A few words about the genesis of this book. Back in 2010, I knuckled under to the increased pressure that a writer *must* have some sort of on-line presence (beyond the required webpage). Since I wanted to make sure I had time to write fiction, I made some rules. I would blog once a week. (By the way, I hate the word "blog," but it seems to have become firmly rooted in the language.) My once-a-week entry would have some substance. I would not write about my socks or my dinner plans or whatever. And I promised myself that I wouldn't feel required to write about writing.

A funny thing happened along the way… I discovered that even when I didn't mean to do so, I often found myself writing about writing. I don't think I realized until I began doing the Wednesday Wanderings just how firmly creating stories was intertwined into just about everything I do.

Eventually, people started saying to me, "You really should collect some of your pieces on writing. They're really interesting and you have a different perspective on a lot of things." Two friends, Bobbi Wolf and Paul Dellinger, were particularly

1

Wanderings on Writing

persistent. When I tentatively mentioned the possibility to my husband, Jim, he encouraged me.

Although many of these pieces have their origins in my Wednesday Wanderings, I've frequently adapted the original essay, providing examples or further discussion of a point. I've omitted specific references to the blog and comments. (If you want to read these, they're still available out on the web.) However, critical readers may discern the shadows.

One thing I did not omit were references to my own work at the time when the piece was written because, in many cases, doing so would have gutted the piece. Although there is a sort of general organization, these pieces do not need to be read in order. Instead, I encourage you to dip in here and there. If a piece is dependent on another, that will be noted. Even where I have several pieces on a related topic, I've chosen to keep them separate. Feel free to read a little, digest the material, then come back for more.

Finally, I will offer a warning. There is no Golden Key to becoming a writer, no secret password, no arcane knowledge that will get you into the inner sanctum. Why do I feel a need to say this?

Years ago, when I received my first invitation to speak at a writer's conference, I consulted another professional writer who was speaking at the same event.

"They've asked me to suggest a topic," I said. "I know how to teach, but I don't really understand what the audience wants." My friend smiled cynically. "They want the Golden Key. They're sure there's one and they've paid this workshop a huge fee in the hope that we will reveal it. All we can do is tell them there isn't any such thing, that writing is hard work, and then share some thoughts about how we go about it."

I don't quite agree with my friend. There is a Golden Key. However, no one can give the Golden Key to you. You need to forge it yourself. That doesn't mean you need to start from nothing. Pieces like the ones in this book can become your raw material. They might save you from building your fire too hot or making your mold from inferior clay.

However, in the end, you need to craft your own Golden Key. One reason I've left the personal anecdotes in here is to show you how I met the challenge.

How Many Pages?

Once upon a time, in very different contexts, I found myself involved in different discussions of the question, "How much do you read of a book before deciding you're not interested?" The amount people gave a novel ranged from a couple of paragraphs to a first chapter. Very rarely was the amount more than three chapters.

The final discussion was with a group of writers. The topic came up not as a matter of craft, but in the context of award judging since many of those present had judged for awards or read slush.

One person's comment seemed to sum up the general feeling: "Well, the thing is, no matter how much you have in front of you, the initial culling goes pretty fast. After all, usually a couple of pages are all you need to know whether it's worth going on."

There were lots of nods around the table and the conversation shifted elsewhere. Afterwards, though, probably because of all those earlier conversations, I found I wasn't comfortable with that easy "Usually a couple of pages are all you need to know whether it's worth going on." Was that really the case?

I decided that while in many cases it was – certainly a few pages would be enough to tell if a piece was poorly written – I wasn't sure I could join those smiling and nodding around the table. Within a relatively short time, I thought of a couple of situations where, if I hadn't read on, I would have missed good reads.

First was Emma Bull's novel *War for the Oaks*. I'd tried this book, but couldn't get past the opening section. Then my buddy David Weber asked if I'd read it. I told him I hadn't and why. He bopped me around the ears (figuratively) and said, "So skip the opening. You'll love that book and you're robbing yourself of a great story." So I skipped the opening section, picked up with the next one and he was right. Not only did I love *War for the Oaks*, I have since recommended it to lots of other people. I also went and hunted up everything else Emma Bull had written.

My other example is more a body of work than a single novel. Terry Pratchett often starts his Discworld novels with a page or two of very strange description of a peculiarly existential nature. If you know the Discworld, this description often provides a foreshadowing of the action to come. However, until I became familiar with the purpose of this section, I often found it off-putting. Now that I know to expect it, however, far from being off-putting, I find it tantalizing, not merely for the foreshadowing but because what is being foreshadowed often seems quite impossible.

Still, these are the exceptions that prove the rule. Especially today, in our sound bite era, most readers won't give a book more than a small sample. How one gets a reader involved is usually termed a narrative hook.

Jane Lindskold

Hooking a Reader

Many years ago, writer Roger Zelazny told me a funny story about narrative hooks.

Roger had been asked to speak at one of the big-name writers' workshops. This workshop was one of the multi-week ones that had two different sets of instructors: the regular faculty who were there for the whole six weeks or so and the guest speakers.

Roger was one of the guest speakers. He came in early in the course and therefore was asked to talk about starting a story. As he told me the tale, he began by explaining to the class how important it was to start a story with something that would grab the reader. Only after the reader was invested in the story should the writer go on and provide the background necessary to understand the events.

He paused, and his co-instructor, a member of the regular faculty, nodded enthusiastically and said, "By all means, let's talk about narrative hooks."

As Roger told it, he looked at her quizzically and said, "All right. What are those?"

He always laughed when he told the story, but I think he also was making a point. No matter how many writer's courses you take, no matter how many trade terms you soak up or how good you are at slinging the jargon, a writer needs to understand the art from inside, not superimpose it from the outside.

Wanderings on Writing

Narrative hooks can take many forms. They might pose a confrontation – whether intellectual or physical. They might drop the reader in the middle of a conversation. They might set the scene – although these days, given the short amount of time most people give a new book, too much artistic scenery description is a good way to lose the reader, unless that reader happens to be in the mood for word paintings.

I've been told that my novel *Marks of Our Brothers* has a great narrative hook. For ease of reference, here it is.

> *My martial arts instructor says that I'm a hopeless cause.*
>
> *"'Do you really want to learn this or is this some kinda joke?' she growls.*
>
> *I don't answer except by hopelessly screwing up another attempt at a breakfall, but I really do want to learn. There are six people that I have to kill and I figure that some idea of how to defend myself might come in handy.*
>
> *Five, I remind myself as I leave the dojo, stiff in body and fatigued from the instructor's impatience.*
>
> *I smile and straighten despite my sore muscles.*
>
> *Five left.*

Why is this a good hook? Well, first of all, it sets up a puzzle. Who is this person and why does she want to kill six other people – even though she is clearly not a professional assassin? The final twist – that she has already succeeded in killing one of her targets – shows that she is very serious about attaining her goal.

One of my personal favorite narrative hooks is from *The Two-Bear Mambo* by Joe Lansdale:

Jane Lindskold

When I got over to Leonard's Christmas Eve night, he had the Kentucky Headhunters turned way up at his place, and they were singing "The Ballad of Davy Crockett," and Leonard, in a kind of Christmas celebration, was once again setting fire to the house next door.

I wished he'd quit doing that. I'd helped him the first time, but he'd done it the second time on his own, and now here I was third time out, driving up. It was going to look damn suspicious when the cops got here.

Does this predict the book's future action? No, but it certainly tells you a lot about the two main characters and their interaction. Right off you know they're close friends. Not only is Christmas Eve the sort of occasion usually shared with dear friends and loved ones, but our narrator admits that the first time Leonard burned down the house, he helped.

This opening also poses an interesting puzzle. I, for one, had to keep reading to find out why Leonard kept burning down the house next door – and why he apparently didn't think he needed to hide his actions. By then I was invested. I kept reading.

Although writers and writers' workshops often present narrative hooks as if a good hook is going to work with every reader at all times, this is far from the case.

I have a good friend, a very intelligent woman with three small children, a family business, and a lot of outside interests. She is also an avid reader. She admits that, at this point in her life, she wants to read books where at least one character is in control of the situation. She doesn't care how wild the ride gets as the story unfolds, as long as she knows that this "control character" will, in the end, set things right.

I admit, I can see her point. If your life is full of chaos, why add more in your down time? I know that at such times, rather than seeking "control characters," I tend to re-read, but the impulse is similar. I know where I'm going. Uncertainty is diminished and so is artificial stress.

Recently, I came across a great example of a narrative hook that would work when I was in one sort of mood, but not in another. It was in the prologue to *Leviathan Wakes* by James S.A. Corey: "The *Scopuli* had been taken eight days ago, and Julie Mao was finally ready to be shot."

I read this, then sat and stared at the page. On the one hand, that sentence caught my curiosity. How could someone be "ready to be shot"? Odd phrase, odd circumstances. On the other hand, the promise of violence, of someone in distress and maybe beyond rescue, made me a little edgy – and I was already in an edgy mood.

Initially, I put the book aside, but a few days later I came back to it and finished the prologue. This ended with what might be considered its own narrative hook.

> An outcropping of the thing shifted toward her. Compared to the whole, it seemed no larger than a toe, a little finger. It was Captain Darren's head.
>
> "Help me," it said.

Well, with that I decided to keep reading. I'll admit, neither of these hooks were what kept me reading to the end of a long novel. My growing interest in the main characters kept me going. Without that, not even the very interesting puzzles presented would have been enough.

However, James S.A. Corey clearly grasped an important part of writing a novel – one hook is not enough. Ideally, each chapter should hook the reader on to the next.

So, how do you decide which sort of narrative hook you want to use? My advice is to be true to the content of the novel. If you start with a sword fight and the rest of the novel is parlor intrigue, you'll disappoint the readers who want action followed by more action. Worse, you'll never attract the readers who thrive on tales based around intricately constructed interpersonal relationships.

If you bait your hook to catch the sort of fish who will swim in your waters, neither you nor they will be disappointed.

How Many Points of View?

Back when I was working my way into *Artemis Invaded*, the sequel to *Artemis Awakening*, I realized that, while *Artemis Awakening* worked just fine with two point-of-view characters, this book demanded a third. Why?

If I tell the honest truth and say because it "felt right," you'd be justified in wanting to roll your eyes in frustration, then jump up and down on my toes. So, although that's perfectly true – I have been writing for publication for over twenty years now, and decisions I once thought my way through have become reflex – I'm going to try to explain a little about the criteria I use to decide how many points of view a book needs.

The first element to consider is what narrative voice I'm using to write. If it's first person ("I"), then I usually stick with one point of view. I have read books that work with two or more "I" narrators, but usually that's not a choice I make. One of the reasons I write first-person is I want to be locked into one point of view. If I feel the book needs more than one point of view, then I shift to third person.

Wanderings on Writing

When I was starting *Through Wolf's Eyes*, I began writing it in first person. I stopped after a relatively short time. Firekeeper's way of seeing the world is so peculiar that I realized that an entire book told solely from her point of view would be maddening.

For those of you who aren't familiar with this book, let me explain that Firekeeper is a human raised by wolves. When the novels starts, she's about fifteen and, as far as she can remember, knows nothing of human culture, customs, or even language. Within the first chapter of the novel, Firekeeper encounters her first humans. She realizes that physically she is more like them than she is like her beloved wolves, but that's where similarities end. Firekeeper doesn't know what a horse is so she thinks of them as like but not like elk, "not elk" for short. She doesn't know what cloth is, so a tent is a double mystery, a sort of portable den made out of material that is and is not like a hide. And so on… You can see why staying tightly within her point of view wouldn't be a good idea.

Therefore, I added Derian's point of view. He knew what horses and tents and stew pots and all sorts of other things were, which was very helpful. As the book progressed and more action started taking place in the royal court – a social sphere nearly as alien to Derian as human society in general was to Firekeeper – Elise, a granddaughter of the king, familiar with those places, stepped in. And so on…

I think of this as a "fan" structure because, as the plot unfolds, so does the number of point-of-view characters. Too often, authors introduce all the point-of-view characters in the first few chapters, whether or not they're needed. This can keep the reader from getting involved with the story, because of all the skipping around for no apparent reason.

Q: So, how many point-of-view characters does a novel need?

A: As many as it needs. Seriously… Some stories need only one point-of-view character. My novel *Child of a Rainless Year* does just fine with only Mira's POV. (Although her adopted mother's journal entries could be considered another point of view, I suppose.) So does *Brother to Dragons, Companion to Owls*. However, after it was published, another author suggested to me that *Marks of our Brothers* (my second published novel) might have benefited from an additional POV. This person felt that the tension could have been heightened if the reader – although not necessarily the characters – had a better idea what the bad guys were plotting.

Maybe so... Certainly, David Weber gets a lot of mileage out of giving the reader both sides of a conflict, so that the reader knows who is planning what and what errors each side is about to make because of ignorance regarding the complexities of the situation. There's definitely an advantage to this choice if building tension is important to the story.

Another reason for more than one POV is to permit "showing" rather than "telling" about various events. A good example of this is Tolkien's novel, *The Two Towers*, where events separated by distance are each told as their own story, rather than having one set reported upon at some later date.

A third great reason for adding additional point-of-view characters is to provide different perspectives on events. As both a reader and a writer, I enjoy becoming immersed in the different ways two people who might be within touching distance perceive the same event or other characters. I play with this a lot in the Firekeeper books.

Here's a great exercise if you want to explore the impact of point of view on a story. Take a section from a book you know well, then retell the action from the different points of view.

Let's use the journey through the Mines of Moria from Tolkien's *The Fellowship of the Ring* as an example. Tolkien tells this mostly from the point of view of an omniscient narrator, although occasionally he dips into Frodo's POV, usually when he wants to add some emotion. Now, sink yourself into each character and tell that section from the different point of view.

Wanderings on Writing

Gimli would be initially optimistic, then apprehensive, then what? Frightened? Vengeful? His point of view of current events would be colored by "I remember when..." "I had hoped..." with every step, every new piece of information.

Gandalf... Does he sense the evil still lurking? Does he realize that they are in a death trap – a death trap that he himself suggested they enter? How does this color his reactions to the place? Remember, he's also the leader, so he's going to be worried about his followers, not just himself.

Legolas? Go beyond the cliché that elves and dwarves don't get along. He's seen the carved door with its hints of old friendship between the races. Would he mull over how time has changed relations? Is this, perhaps, the turning point in his own relationship with Gimli?

How about the humans? How do they feel about these dwarven tunnels? Cramped? Claustrophobic? Do they feel their relative youth as a race? Would Boromir and Aragorn think the same way? Why not? How would these differences color how they see precisely the same place?

The Hobbits would probably be delighted to be underground, yet frightened by the death and destruction surrounding them. Again, would Frodo, with his greater education and sense of history, see things differently from the younger hobbits? How would Sam's soul – so romantic, yet so practical – color his view of the place? How about Merry and Pippin? Does their reaction go beyond relief at being out of the snow? Do their reactions differ from each other in any way?

These variations in reaction are among the reasons I usually prefer writing from the point of view of one or more characters, rather than from that of an omniscient narrator. Point of view can add richness and spice. It can add character to events that otherwise could become nothing more than plodding plot. Like any spice, point of view should be handled with precision and care but, without it, I find that the most exciting story can become bland.

The Beating Heart of a Story

Leaving out conflict is a mistake many beginning writers make. They have an image in their minds and think that verbally presenting that image or writing an anecdote about the characters is a story. This limited presentation may work for a visual image – but it isn't enough for a story. At the very best, you may end up with a vignette – but a vignette is not a story.

(*Webster's Third New International Dictionary* defines a written vignette as: "a short literary sketch chiefly descriptive and characterized usu. by delicacy, wit, and subtlety.")

By conflict I don't mean sword fights, shoot-outs, or car chases. Those are just the physical outgrowths of conflict. Two quotations illustrate this beautifully. Carl von Clausewitz said: "War is the continuation of politics by other means." Zhou Enlai memorably riffed off of this with: "All diplomacy is a continuation of war by other means." In other words, you can have lots of conflict without a single sword being drawn or shot fired.

(In fact, you can have shots fired and swords drawn and no conflict at all – for example, in a training or practice session.)

There are three basic forms conflict can take in a story. In sexist days of yore, the three types of conflict were termed "man against man," man against self," and "man against nature." That's still a pretty good shorthand, if you understand "man" to mean "intelligent, sentient entity," which is a real mouthful. "Person against person" doesn't have the same ring, and the alteration sounds even worse with "person against self." "Human against human" is a dangerous limitation for those of us who write SF/F. So, for the nonce, let's stick with "man."

(Seriously, I worked over these with a word-loving friend for quite a while. The best alternative we could come up with was "individual" and that just lacks the snap. I'm open to suggestions!)

"Man against man" superficially seems pretty obvious. Your protagonist is competing against a person or persons, right? Most people immediately envision stories involving physical contests, battles, or the like. However, "man against man" conflict isn't limited to arena fights or races. A detective tracking down a murderer or thief is involved in a "man against man" conflict. Two people competing for the same promotion or love interest would be "man against man" stories. War stories – no matter how high tech – are still "man against man" stories.

An interesting twist on the "man against man" conflict is when a character has a secret and someone else wants to learn it. Secret identities create immediate conflict because the one with the secret has something to lose if the secret is revealed. However, more subtle secrets work, too. In her Stephanie Plum novels, Janet Evanovich creates a lot of tension – and occasional humor – around Stephanie's continuing search to learn more about Ranger.

Evanovich is very skillful at raising the ante. Every time Stephanie learns something about Ranger, she realizes there is more to learn. Remember this if you want to use a secret of any sort to create conflict or tension in a story. Once it's known, it no longer serves.

Jane Lindskold

"Man against nature" conflict goes far beyond the struggle to be the first to climb a mountain or reach the South Pole or kill the ferocious dragon or man-killing tiger. (In fact, if the dragon is intelligent, then the story is actually a variation on a "man against man" conflict.) Any time characters need to struggle to overcome a physical challenge, you have a man against nature conflict.

Frodo and Sam laboring to cross Mordor, then to climb that interminable stair... Jack Aubrey struggling to sail the *Surprise* through a keel-cracking storm... Gully Foyle putting on a patched space suit to venture into vacuum to gather bottled air and supplies... These are just a few examples of memorable "man against nature" conflicts.

One way to differentiate "man against nature" conflicts from "man against man" conflicts is that the opponent is either non-thinking or restricted to a limited "animal" cunning. A storm doesn't care if it sinks the ship – no matter how much the sailors personify it or blame bad luck or whatever. A man-eating tiger just wants a chance at an easy dinner. It's only humans who decide the tiger is on a vendetta to get even for a burned paw.

"Man against self" is the sort of conflict that changes a cardboard character into a three-dimensional human being. SF in particular is prone to one-dimensional characters – in part because SF is the home of the "idea story." In too many idea stories, the characters become nothing but props for the exploration of that idea.

Fantasy and Mystery share with SF the great danger of characters being reduced to "types" – and not just mythic archetypes, but characters right out of central casting: the burly barbarian warrior; the sly, silent thief; the wise wizard stroking his long beard as he expounds some bit of lore; the tough detective whose weary eyes have seen too much; the gangster, street-smart, but curiously naïve; the prostitute with a heart of gold...

Giving these characters some internal conflict makes them more real – and provides some interesting potential plot twists. What if your burly barbarian warrior is terrified of fire because he saw his family burned alive? What happens when he confronts a flame-belching dragon? Will he crumple or will his strong sense of duty to his companions keep him going? What about a thief who, rather than being sly, is perfectly direct about why he turned to crime – and who hopes to earn enough money to run for parliament and set the social order right?

Dorothy L. Sayers' Lord Peter Wimsey is a great example of not only a character, but an entire series, being defined by a "man against self" conflict. Peter suffers badly from shell-shock. (They hadn't invented the term "PTSD" then. Anyhow, his problem actually is related to shelling and trench warfare.) When he returns to civilian life, he copes by focusing on various hobbies – the most absorbing of which is solving crimes. As the series progresses, Peter recovers somewhat, but he never gets over a certain guilt that he is sending men to the gallows to distract himself from his own personal horrors.

Take care not to overweight your character with too many problems. Not only do you risk alienating your reader, you risk turning your character into someone incapable of acting – or worse, a parody. This last is fine if parody is your intention but, if you had hoped to create a tragic, Byronic figure who has turned to drink and is incapable of commitment, and instead end up with someone the readers see as a self-obsessed drunk who runs through girlfriends as fast as he does bottles of cheap gin…

Overweighting the character with internal conflicts isn't as much a problem in SF and Fantasy, where rich world-building and complex challenges provide a balance, but I'm seeing it more and more in Mystery fiction.

A wonderful story that features all three forms of conflict is Roger Zelazny's "The Doors of His Face, The Lamps of His Mouth." Carl is a baitman, a sort of fishing guide, on a Venus where the prize of big game hunters is Ichthyform Leviosaurus Levianthus – a huge aquatic creature usually called "Ikky" for short.

Jane Lindskold

When the story starts, Carl's a not-quite out-of-control drunk for reasons initially left vague, though it's hinted that whatever is wrong with him has something to do with a past encounter with Ikky. So, within a few pages, Zelazny presents "man against nature" and "man against self." "Man against man" enters with Jean Luharich, who not only turns out to be Carl's next client, but his ex-wife.

Something for everyone... and Zelazny ties all three together at the end, which is the most satisfying of all. There's a good reason this story won the Hugo Award for Best Novelette in 1966. Or at least that's how I see it!

False Conflict

(Before you read this piece, you might want to glance at "The Beating Heart of a Story.")

There's a hidden flaw that undermines many a story. This is what I call the False Conflict.

Let me give an example... Your story features Valor, a knight – good and loyal and true. Valor's a little past his prime, although he's still a good fighter. He has risen to be a commander of armies. Throughout his long career, Valor has remained true to his code. Unfortunately, for him, the monarch he serves has changed over time. King has become paranoid, worried about threats to his power, and generally unpleasant.

When our story begins, King is at war with the neighboring Foe.

17

Wanderings on Writing

Foe is known for treating his soldiers well. He is powerful, but not abusive of his power. In the course of battle, Valor is wounded and taken prisoner by Foe's forces. He comes around to find his wounds treated and that he is housed in a nice room. Eventually, Foe summons Valor. He offers Valor a place in his chain of command – though not at the top, because that would be unfair to his own faithful retainers. Will Valor accept?

In the story as defined, there is no real conflict – neither "man against man" nor "man against self." Why not? Because Valor is presented as the good knight and true. He has no other life. In the course of the story, he doesn't snap back at the rude and ungrateful King. He never thinks about leaving or retiring. He forges on. In our guts, we know he will turn down Foe, so what should be a dramatic ending is hollow.

(And, yes, people do write stories like this. A lot.)

However, introduce some "man against self" conflict into the story and everything changes. The reader turns pages with a wildly thumping heart, eager to learn which way Valor will go. The alternatives build. Maybe Valor will agree to join Foe – but secretly plan to be a double agent. Maybe Valor actually believes that Foe would be a better ruler, and realizes his loyalty is not to King, but to the kingdom. Maybe Valor will refuse to join Foe and spend the rest of the war in prison, constantly doubting that he has made the right choice.

A great example of a novel that uses "man against self" conflict to add dimension to what otherwise could have become a standard adventure story is Walter Jon Williams' *Hardwired*. When *Hardwired* begins, Sarah's main goal is to earn enough money to get herself and her brother, Daud, off-planet, into one of the orbital habitats. She has good reason. Daud has a drug addiction that will kill him if she can't get him away. Sarah feels she must save Daud – no matter how tough or ugly the jobs she has to do to earn the money. In the course of doing these jobs, Sarah learns of a group that's trying to overthrow the system that has created this stratified (literally, as well as economically) society. She's pulled toward them and their cause, but joining them would mean giving up her efforts to save Daud. The first time I read *Hardwired*, I wasn't sure which way Sarah would go.

So, what about those Mystery stories where you know, even before you start reading, that the detective will solve the murder? Didn't I say that a detective chasing a murderer is an example of "man against man" conflict? So, shouldn't I really have said that these were examples of False Conflict?

Not at all. First of all, Mystery novels aren't just about "whodunit." They're often about "whydunit" and "can we prove it?" The television show *Columbo* demonstrated very effectively that you can have a Mystery story where the reader (in this case, viewer) knows the solution before the characters do. The pleasure is in how the mystery is solved – and, oddly enough, the sense of tension is even higher.

As I mentioned in "How Many Points of View?", a great way to add tension to a story is to provide the reader with information the characters don't have. Rather than diminishing conflict, it drives up the sense of drama, as well as adding complexity to the plot. David Weber does this very well in his sprawling space operas, with the added benefit of creating a sense of identification with both sides of the conflict. This is particularly important to increasing reader involvement when – as Weber frequently does – you have a novel with a large cast of characters, too many of whom could become faceless, cardboard pawns.

"Man against nature" is one of the easiest ways to fall into False Conflict. Journeys often occur in SF and Fantasy stories. However, whether through the dark reaches of outer space or through forests and over mountains, they should serve a purpose. Otherwise, they are simply filler – implying a "man against nature" challenge but not really delivering – especially since the reader knows deep down inside that what happens at the journey's end, not the journey itself, is what's important.

Wanderings on Writing

Especially if you write SF or Fantasy, here's a helpful trick. Take your journey and mentally translate it into another genre. Mystery is a good one to use, because journeys for the sake of the journey rarely have a part. (Even the *Murder on the Orient Express* is more characterized for the journey being unexpectedly halted, than the journey itself.) If your journey doesn't serve beyond getting your characters from point A to point B, then do as a Mystery writer would and truncate it down to a few lines.

Don't get me wrong. There are journeys that serve many purposes – introducing the setting, providing opportunities for characterization, inserting future complications – but if you're just slogging the characters along, maybe with a little fight or two to liven up the trip, then it's filler. Cut it and get to the real conflict. You'll have more fun and your readers will thank you.

"Plotting On"

I don't participate in NaNoWriMo or writer's boot camps or any of those gimmicks meant to get people over the "Someday when I have time, I have a great idea for a novel" stage and into actively writing. That doesn't mean I don't enjoy hearing about people's ventures into these areas.

One thing that often comes up is that, once the story was started, the writers frequently found themselves getting bogged down. Matters of plot and characterization that had seemed obvious at the start of the race or workshop no longer seemed so clear once the pressure to produce on a daily basis was there. However, for a professional writer, regular production is a requirement.

Jane Lindskold

So, how does one keep going once the novel is started, the main characters introduced, and that boffo narrative hook written? Here are a few tricks I use.

My first suggestion is more a matter of structuring your writing time than of stimulating creativity. Stop writing in the middle of the scene, when you know exactly where you're going. It's best to choose a dramatic point – fights or passionate conversations are both good. If you're worried that you'll lose the momentum you've developed, write yourself brief notes, rather like the following: [Firekeeper next disagrees; Derian comes back with timing issue; Firekeeper sees point; next, depart on trip]

I usually put these notes in square brackets because one typically doesn't use them for anything else, so they're easy to search for and remove.

Second, if you find yourself bogged down regarding matters of plot, consider your problem in this light. You're bogged down because there's more than one possible "next." For example, you know your protagonist is going to end up face to face with the antagonist. From the start, you knew that your protagonist would win this first encounter. So what's the problem?

The problem is that, even if you know your protagonist is the victor in this particular confrontation, there are so many different types of victories – especially if the antagonist needs to continue to play a role in the story. Let's set up a hypothetical situation and see where it takes us.

(This technique is called brainstorming. You don't need to write everything out to effectively brainstorm. In fact, it's often best if you don't. Just pull out some scrap paper or an old notebook and start scribbling fragments. That way you don't get bogged down by trying to come up with perfect prose.)

Okay. Here's our situation. Our novel is centered around the ongoing conflict between two heroes: Ace of Hearts and Black

Wanderings on Writing

Spade. As we initially envisioned it, in the first encounter between Ace of Hearts and Black Spade, Ace wins. Simple, right? But remember what I said about different types of victories.

Here are a few possibilities I came up with right off the top of my head:

> 1) Ace of Hearts wins, but it's a qualified victory. Maybe she's wounded. Maybe complications spring up – perhaps local law enforcement becomes involved.

> 2) Ace of Hearts wins but, in order to do so, she had to pull out her "big guns" (which could be a spell or other device or even an ally, as easily as a weapon) earlier than she planned. Black Spade is defeated, but escapes with this valuable information. Especially if Ace counted on keeping that bit of information a secret, she may feel this is a mixed victory.

> 3) Ace wins. The Black Spade is dead or in prison. However, a lieutenant – the Crimson Club – now takes over and is worse than the Spade ever was. Or the Marked Deck Gang decides to rescue the boss. Or the Black Spade turns out to be a real charmer and pretty soon local law enforcement is convinced they have the wrong person behind bars.

I'm sure you can think of other alternatives. The point is, the reason you're stuck is because you're aware that there are consequences to any action. This is situation is one that most new writers aren't prepared for. They figure knowing the general plot is enough. If they outline, they may have confidently written something like: "First Encounter between Ace of Hearts and Black Spade. Ace wins." They didn't think hard enough about how Ace won and what that victory would mean to the larger story.

A third option for when you find yourself getting bogged down once the book is underway is to toss that outline. Outlines are meant to help you. If you find yours becoming a shackle on your creativity, then do some rethinking. Try writing a new approach or two, then decide which of these new angles you like best and continue from there.

Related to this is a problem that most experienced writers are familiar with, but neo writers don't believe is real until it happens to them. This is when the characters hijack the book and start taking the plot in another direction. Maybe you'd predicated a lot of the action on Character A being deeply in love with Character B. Then Character A turns out to be indifferent to Character B, but is flirting with Character C.

Or maybe, as noted above, you planned on the first confrontation ending in victory for the protagonist. Instead, when you start writing, the antagonist keeps coming up with all these great ways for escaping the protagonist's carefully-laid plans. Yeah, you can force the plot to go as you originally intended, but you might end up with a much stronger book if you find out where this side road takes you. That road is possibly a dead end, but even that investigation will teach you something about your characters and how they react to adversity.

The strangest thing of all is that very often, once you've solved your problem and the plot is moving along nicely once more, the solution seems so obvious that you wonder why you didn't think of it from the start. Then, if you're like some writers I know, you begin to wonder if what you have come up with is too dumb or too obvious. Trust yourself. It probably isn't.

One of my hobbies is role-playing games. Often, when I set up my notes for an adventure (all of mine are original stories), I say to Jim, "Gee, I hope this isn't going to be too direct and too boring for you all." Usually, as we are cleaning up after a session, Jim looks at me and grins, "Didn't you say you were worried this would be too direct and too boring? Let me reassure you... It's not!"

Wanderings on Writing

So my last piece of advice is this. Even when you're in doubt, keep writing. Feel free to go in new directions, but don't throw away everything you've done to that point because you're momentarily stuck. Keep going. You won't know how well – or how poorly – the story has turned out until you're finished.

Reverse Outlining

Q: Reverse outlining? What are you talking about? And, hey, wait! Aren't you always saying you don't outline your novels?

A: You're right. I do say that and I hold to it. I don't outline a novel before writing it – which is what most people mean when they talk about outlining – but I do outline as I write. Often I start when I have a chapter or two in place.

Q: Why would you bother to outline what you've already written? I mean, isn't it wasted effort? Don't you have the manuscript there in front of you?

A: I do have it and, no, it's not wasted effort. In fact, I find reverse outlining the absolutely best way for me to keep track of my plot, characters, and the general flow of the action in an evolving novel.

Q: So, how does reverse outlining work?

A: First, I pull out a sheaf of nice, white lined paper. Yes. I could do this on a computer, but I'm one of those people who remembers things better if I write them down by hand. Since part of the goal of a reverse outline is to serve as an aid to memory, I write mine by hand.

Next, I pull out a sheaf of brightly-colored pens. I assign one color to each point-of-view character and another to be used for chapter headings. I also pull out a pencil. The last preparatory step is to pull the manuscript file up on my computer screen.

Since my reverse outline isn't for anyone except me, I don't worry about writing down everything that happens in a particular section. I focus in on events that will jog my memory when questions crop up like "When exactly did they arrive in Spirit Bay?" or "When did that mugging happen?" or "How many days have elapsed since…."

In the side margin I use the pencil to note what day a given event happened. I use pencil because sometimes dates shift, especially if I end up going and adding something later on. If the book has a precise starting date, I use that. Otherwise, I simply label each day as Day One, Day Two, etc. Later on, I can always add a notation as to calendar date, if that will be important. I also make notations as to season, since time of year can affect anything from length of days to temperature. I note the phase of the moon if that will be important – as it often is in adventures set outdoors.

Q: What do you do if the action skips ahead several days?

A: I make a note of that as well. More importantly, I note *why* those days were skipped. Maybe there was uneventful travel or maybe time needed to heal from a wound or maybe the characters were waiting for some information. Especially in the case of travel time, these details can come in really useful, making sure that journeys between points take about the same amount of time.

I recently finished reading a Fantasy novel in which I never could feel the terrain was real, since travel time between points seemed to shift according to the needs of the plot. Most of the novel, the characters seemed to slog along, step by step. However, when the climax required a last-minute arrival of the Good Guys, they showed up, a bit sweaty and all, but certainly faster than I could believe. It took some of the fun out of the climax for me to feel that there was a *deus ex machina*, when the plot was going out of its way to eliminate *deus* or *machina*.

Yes, I do realize that, especially when a book is set in a low-tech setting, travel times can vary widely. If so, why not make a note of the reason? You don't need to write that long slog through the snow unless that slog is important, but you can note that getting from point A to point B took more or less time because of weather conditions.

Q: Are there any other reasons that you reverse outline?

A: You bet! Reverse outlining can help with characterization, too. Characters can marvel that they've known each other only a few days, but feel bonded. Or, conversely, that they've been together for weeks but, after a short time, the friendship ceased to progress beyond initial introductions.

Q: Why do you color-code your point-of-view characters?

A: Well, beyond the fact that it gives me an excuse to play with colored pens, which I love, I do this because it enables me to see at a glance whether the story has gotten out of balance.

Certainly, there are times when one character has more to do than another. However, writers can become deeply drawn into one plot thread at the expense of another. If this isn't deliberate, then some rebalancing is in order.

Using different colored pens shows me, literally at a glance, when this sort imbalance is happening.

I've told many people about reverse outlining. What's interesting to me is that, even for writers who outline in the more traditional sense, the technique can be useful. One person I know set up side by side outlines, so he could see where the story he was writing had diverged from the one he had outlined. In this way, he could see if he missed a key point and needed to work it in.

So, whether you're an intuitive plotter, like me, or one who plans in advance, reverse outlining can be surprisingly useful.

How Much Back Story Do You Need?

Over Christmas, I broke down and decided to try the second part of *SaiYuki* in manga form. *SaiYuki* (despite its flaws) is one of my favorite anime. I like the manga, too, but – as is not uncommon in this form – the two storylines diverge. [1]

The second part of *SaiYuki* is called *SaiYuki: Reload*. I was turned off by the anime immediately. Moreover, none of the reviews I read early on encouraged me to make the investment in time to see if it improved. Occasionally, I'd wistfully pick up a DVD and read the back... Eventually, I noticed that they were now re-telling the tale that had been the second part of the manga...

So if the anime of *Reload* was using part of the story from the original manga, what the heck did the manga of *SaiYuki: Reload* include?

---

[1]   Manga are often termed "Japanese comic books." This isn't really accurate. They're illustrated stories, but that's where the similarity ends. They're written for all age levels, and feature a wide variety of stories. Anime are the animated versions of the illustrated story. Anime may or may not be based on an existing manga.

Wanderings on Writing

I decided to find out. Within two issues, I realized that I was going to like this story. One thing I had loved about *SaiYuki* was that the characters had rich back stories... both in their current lives and in a shared incarnation five hundred years in the past. *SaiYuki: Reload* continued to move the present-day storyline forward while delving into past events – including a tie between the beloved teacher of one of the main characters and the enigmatic Dr. Ni.

Anyhow, all of this got Jim and me talking about how much we both enjoy a degree of back story. Done well, it adds so much to the characters and to the story at large. A good example is Rex Stout's stories about Nero Wolfe. Most of the time, those tales are simply good detective stories but, occasionally, as in *Over My Dead Body* and *The Black Mountain*, you learn about Nero Wolfe's past...

That past changes Nero Wolfe from a contrived eccentric, clearly indebted to Mycroft Holmes (Sherlock Holmes' smarter brother), to a rich and vivid character in his own right. As much as I like Agatha Christie, I wish she'd done something like this with Miss Marple. In Miss Marple's case, except for occasional superficial references, Jane Marple is a woman without a past, always old, always curiously wise.

But there can be too much back story. I just finished a very long novel in which no character, no matter how minor, is presented without a long biographical sketch. At first I tried to remember these, thinking they would be important. Then I realized they were nothing but fat... The author had come up with these character bios, they had gotten onto the page, and – probably because this author is very popular – no one had the guts to tell him to take them off.

Right after that, I re-read Andre Norton's *Star Gate*. In contrast to my previous read, especially in matters of character, *Star Gate* almost seemed like the outline for a novel. The characters weren't cardboard or pawns for the action but, except for the protagonist, very little of the pasts of the other characters made it onto the page. In some ways, this fit the book – Kincar is very much out of place and is the last person to start prying – but I wished Andre Norton had included a little more about the others.

So, how much back story do you want to include in your novel?

One thing you should consider is what the back story will contribute to the tale you're telling. If it won't do much, then a few brushstrokes to make your character more real are enough. However, if it's crucial to the story, then you should be prepared to present it.

No matter how important that back story is, make certain you have your reader hooked before you start presenting it. In my *Through Wolf's Eyes*, I could have started the novel with Earl Kestrel putting together his expedition to search for the missing Prince Barden. I could have gone even further back, and explained the complicated political situation that had left House Kestrel a minor player in the contest for the soon-to-be vacant throne.

Instead, I started with Firekeeper hearing the wolves howling to announce the arrival of "strangers strange." Only later, and in small installments, does the reader learn who those strangers are and why they made the journey. By then, I hoped the reader would care. As for Firekeeper's own history, that takes even longer to be revealed.

Back story is important, but it should be presented when the reader will be eager for it, not as a dull history lesson to be slogged through before getting to the "real" story.

Wanderings on Writing

Luck and Coincidence

Just how much luck can a story take?

We all accept a certain amount of luck – or luck's close cousin, "coincidence" – in our daily lives. Indeed, people enjoy sharing stories of when luck seemed to play a part – especially for the good, but even when the outcome was bad. Perhaps we like these tales because luck (or coincidence) seems to hint at a larger pattern of purpose in a universe that has come to seem increasingly purposeless.

Ah... But I become too philosophical.

In the not-so-distant past, an author could get away with using coincidence to move along the plot. The protagonist might overhear a conversation which warned him or her of a sinister plot or revealed that someone whom he (or she) had thought was a friend was actually not as favorably disposed as the protagonist had believed.

Sometimes, this overheard information might prove to be flawed. Especially in romance novels, the heroine frequently seems to be in a position to see her beloved embracing a beautiful woman before glancing up and down the street and slipping into a nearby house. Of course, later you learn this woman was his sister or cousin or whatever, but the plot has been jiggered along with a new complication.

Jane Lindskold

There's a lovely bit in C.S. Lewis's *Voyage of the Dawn Treader* where, via the agency of a magical book, Lucy overhears a girl she thought was her friend saying unkind things about her to another girl. Lucy is – quite understandably – shocked and hurt. Later, however, she learns that the friend had only spoken as she had because she feared the other girl. This scene provides not only a nice reminder about the dangers of eavesdropping, but also a hint that events are often more complex than we imagine.

As even genre fiction writing became more sophisticated, situations such as the villain neatly outlining his entire plan to conquer the world when the protagonist is in a position to hear the details and so foil the villain's nefarious schemes, became regarded as so contrived and unlikely as to become a matter of humor.

Towards the end of Roger Zelazny's *Prince of Chaos*, Merlin (not the Merlin of Arthurian legend, just someone with the same name), waits in a room off a long corridor to avoid an approaching group of people. Merlin thinks, "In a badly plotted story they'd have paused outside the doorway, and I would have overheard a conversation telling me everything I needed to know about anything." They don't, of course. In fact, what Merlin overhears is so banal as to be less than useless.

I enjoyed Jacqueline Winspear's post-WWI historical novel *Maisie Dobbs*. However, there was a sequence early in the novel that nearly kept me from reading further. Maisie has newly set herself up in business as a private investigator. In a tremendous bit of luck, she meets up with a war veteran who had his life and his leg saved by the surgeon Maisie was assisting. (She'd been a nurse during the war.)

Not only does Billy remember Maisie, but he is so intensely grateful that he offers to assist with little jobs about her office. Moreover, he turns out to have the exact combination of skills and traits necessary to help Maisie solve her first important solo case. Had the book not been recommended by someone whose taste I trust, as soon as I saw how large a role coincidence was going to play, I might not have finished reading.

And yet... Would I have been right to do so?

Is the ruling out of coincidence as an element in a story's plot entirely fair? Plans do get overheard – especially if the protagonist is already suspicious and therefore searching for opportunities to learn more. I believe that there is documentation that even more unlikely occurrences – such as a pocket Bible or lucky silver coin stopping a bullet – have happened.

I have a good friend who is a retired reporter. Back when he was still on the beat, his letters often included little oddities he encountered as he raced from one location to another. I remember one in particular. He'd been running behind getting somewhere because an interview ran long. On the way to his next appointment, he was slowed further by a major highway accident. As he waited for the traffic to clear, my friend found himself realizing that if he'd been on time, he likely would have been even later, because his car would have been at the heart of the accident.

"But if I put that in a story, no one would believe it."

My general rule of thumb is to limit myself to one major coincidence or lucky incident in a book. Kept to this limited use, oddly enough, it can make a plot seem more real. I don't use luck or coincidence for anything that will resolve a major crisis within the story, but if a certain huntress happens to be in the general vicinity when a shuttle crashes... Well, that kicks off the story and the rest is history!

Jane Lindskold

What's in a Name?

My parents thought they were doing me a favor when they named me Jane. My dad felt that "Lindskold" was enough of a name to saddle any kid with and suggested short first names. (Dad and his sisters were Ruth, John, and Mary, so I suspect he was following his own parents' lead in this).

As I understand it, Dad also favored naming his first kid for himself. Out of all the possible feminine forms of "John," he and Mom chose "Jane" in honor of two of Mom's close friends.

However, my name, simple as it was, proved a continual source of trouble. I was called "plain Jane," taunted with "Hey, Jane, having fun with Dick?" (A taunt that took on a sexual edge once I realized what "dick" might be). I was repeatedly asked "Hey, Jane. Where's Tarzan?" This last was always followed with howling and chest-thumping in the best movie Tarzan tradition.

I longed for a cool nickname. No luck. When I was in high school, I started spelling my name "Jayne" – as if that would make a difference. (I kept doing this through college, but began to drop the practice, except for friends, once I was publishing – my first publications were academic and pen names weren't part of the picture.)

I thought about the impact of names the other day while I was digging through baby books, dictionaries, and other sources, looking for just the right names for several characters. There are various guidelines I have set for myself.

Wanderings on Writing

Names should be relatively easy to pronounce. If names have a meaning, I should be aware of it. If I'm using a "cute" variant spelling, I need to know why the character's parents chose it.

I try not to have too many character names start with the same few letters to avoid confusing fast readers who tend to skim and read by shape. (As I myself do.) Sometimes I don't follow this last rule. In *Five Odd Honors*, you'll meet a character named "Parnell." This name is close in "shape" to "Pearl," but I liked both names and decided they were different enough that I could live with the similarity of that initial P and final L.

Names can shape a character. Gaheris Morris in *Thirteen Orphans* was originally "Garrett." My friend Chris Krohn came to a reading from the unfinished novel (something I rarely do). Afterwards, Chris told me there was a comedian with a very similar name. The general sound of the name was already in my head, so I didn't want to change it too much. I came up with Gaheris. Then I had to ask myself what sort of mother would name her child after a Knight of the Round Table. So a complex character background was born – one with consequences for Gaheris's daughter, Brenda.

Sometimes characters' personal histories will shape the name I give them. Firekeeper's "baby name" was "Little Two-legs" because, to the wolves who raised her, the fact that she walked on two legs was her most distinguishing feature. The fact that she qualified for the "adult name" of Firekeeper says a lot about how the wolves now viewed their human foster child - despite Firekeeper's own insecurities regarding how weak, "nose dead," and otherwise inferior she is to the wolves.

It's all great fun.

You know, now that I think about it, my parents did do me a favor naming me "Jane." Not only did I spend a lot of time thinking about names, but also those taunts led me to reading books I might not otherwise have discovered. One day at a flea market when I was in about sixth grade, I came across a box of yellowed Tarzan novels.

After initially flinching to find my nemesis here as well, I was tempted. I bought a couple books for a nickel apiece. I loved them. Next time someone said, "Hey, Jane. Where's Tarzan?" I began babbling. Did they know that Tarzan was an English lord? That he could talk to animals? That he had this really big knife? That he was *so* cool.

Funny. The teasing stopped. A little knowledge is a dangerous thing.

Long and Winding Names

Earlier this week, I had an e-mail from a friend who is a long-time SF/F reader asking the following question: "Why is it that some writers like to make up long names consisting of many, many consonants with maybe two or three vowels? They are completely unpronounceable. When I see them I frown. I recently started reading such a book, gave up and threw it away. What's wrong with names that sound normal?"

While I've touched on names before (in "What's in a Name?"), there's certainly room to expand.

Obviously, I can't answer for every writer. Although long names and terms are not something I use often, I have done it, especially when establishing a different culture. In *Wolf Captured*, Firekeeper, Blind Seer, and Derian end up in the country of Liglim.

Wanderings on Writing

The language of Liglim is agglutinative – that is, shorter words combine to make longer ones (as is the case in many Germanic languages, including English, and in Japanese).

Since I wanted to make sure readers would know how to pronounce the words, I used a modified phonetic spelling. Therefore, for the character "Harjeedian," I used "ee" rather than "I" in the second syllable, so there would be no confusion. However, for the final syllable, I did not feel the need to use a double "e" instead of an 'I' because in the "ia" combination with that consonant the "I" is usually pronounced rather like a long "e."

Equally, for "Rahniseeta," I used "ah" rather than just "a" for the first syllable, so there would be no question as to whether the sound indicated was a long or short "a." Having, hopefully, established that in most cases a single "I" is pronounced as a short "I," I left that, but used a double "e" in the second to last syllable.

This seems to have worked, because readers who have spoken to me about the characters usually pronounce the names correctly. Oddly enough, it is the short word "Liglim," that causes problems. I've heard it pronounced "Lee-gleem," "Lee-glim," Lig-gleem," and, correctly, "Lig-lim." So, obviously, shorter is not always clearer!

Ironically, the cover copy for *Wolf Captured* made up an entirely new word: Liglimoshti. This frustrated me quite a bit, since within the novel the culture is always referred to as the Liglimom. Ah, well... Just goes to prove the old saying, "Never judge a book by its cover copy."

I want to go back to one part of the question that started all of this: "What's wrong with names that sound normal?"

To this I answer, "What is normal?"

I live in New Mexico, which is officially bilingual (Spanish and English). I am so accustomed to seeing election ballots and other official documents printed in both English and Spanish that I'd find it "abnormal" to see a ballot that didn't include both languages.

Street names and place names go back and forth with cheerful lack of rhyme or reason between languages. There's one street that is Montaño (Spanish for "mountain") for part of its length and then shifts to Montgomery. I suppose someone who didn't know any Spanish could be forgiven for thinking Montaño meant "Montgomery," but I'm willing to bet that most people who live here know that it doesn't.

This takes me to the problem of writing a book that uses another extant culture. I've run into this quite a few times, most particularly in *Legends Walking*, part of which takes place in Nigeria, and in the "Breaking the Wall" series (first book, *Thirteen Orphans*) in which many of the characters are either Chinese or of Chinese descent.

English is commonly spoken in Nigeria, so I was fine there. However, both from reading novels set in Nigeria and non-fiction about the region, I rapidly learned that Nigerian English was heavily salted with terms from many languages spoken by the various ethnic/linguistic groups that reside within the borders. I chose to follow the same custom, doing my best to carefully define terms within context.

However, this choice meant that I had to deal with the problem of accent marks. (See "Accent on Page" if you're interested in knowing how I dealt with this issue.)

The "Breaking the Wall" books provided an entirely different challenge. Not only isn't there one accepted way to transliterate Chinese, the "accepted" pronunciations often reflect the domination of Northern Chinese over the other dialects. People around my age or older probably remember when we were told that "Peking" was now "Beijing" – and that the name had not been changed, just how it was to be spelled and pronounced.

Wanderings on Writing

In preparation for writing the "Breaking the Wall" novels, I performed an informal experiment and learned something very interesting. Readers unfamiliar with the base language have more trouble "seeing" a foreign word, especially one that is oddly pronounced. In a novel about Chinese characters in which the names were given in Chinese, I had more trouble remembering the names than I did when the names were partly or completely translated. So "Master Li" or "Judge Dee" would stay in my mind, whereas "Qu Boyu" and "Zhongni" did not.

I asked around and found this was the case for many people. Therefore, deciding that my job as a writer was to communicate, not to provide a language lesson, most of the time I gave the translations for the names, rather than making my readers learn another language and its conventions. This choice also saved me from having to decide which transliteration version to use. Not having to deal with whether to change the transliteration according to dialect, or whether the character was from "The Land of the Burning" (our world) or "The Land Born of Smoke and Sacrifice" (the alternate China), was a bonus.

Remember, familiarity with a language changes everything. Writers need to remember that they may have been working within their invented language, or within another culture for long enough that what was once odd has become familiar. However, this will not be the case for the reader.

Back when I taught college, during one term I had several Japanese exchange students in one class. Three of these were named Yumiko, Yukiko, and Yukari. I despaired of ever getting their names right but, within a month, I had no problem. However, it did occur to me that I would not have even thought about having trouble remembering the names if my students had been named "Ann," "Andrea," and "Angela." It was the combination of the unfamiliar first letter "Y" (not very common in English – and even names like "Yvonne" and "Yvette" are often mispronounced) and my lack of familiarity with Japanese.

In the years since, I have learned a lot more Japanese and probably wouldn't have the same problem. "Yukiko," for example, would automatically break down into "yuki" (snow) and "ko" (a common feminine suffix, roughly translated as "child").

So, to answer my friend's question, what is unpronounceable may not be unpronounceable, what is normal may not be normal, but a writer should never forget that writing is communication and you owe your readers some consideration.

Accent on the Page

Recently, I was reading a book where one of the non-human races was stated to have a distinct accent. However, the author never did anything to make that accent come across. Moreover, it was not described in any concrete fashion, so I couldn't imagine what was intended.

That got me thinking about the entire question – maybe even problem – of accents, dialects, and the like in SF/F. How far should a writer go when putting these on the page? At what point does the reader simply scream "Enough! I get the idea!!!"

I started fishing about in my imagination for examples of when accents had been done well. For convenience, let's include dialects, colloquialisms, slang, and general cadence under the term "accent," since I think "accent" is often more than how sounds are articulated.

Wanderings on Writing

Tolkien did a good job in his Middle Earth novels. Sam and Frodo are both hobbits, but their choice of vocabulary is different, making it clear they are of different social classes. Elves and dwarves speak differently than humans. A light sprinkling of their own languages helps show minds that process concepts differently. Even the three trolls in *The Hobbit* speak in a distinct manner.

Much as I like attention to how characters speak, I do find myself going a little nuts when there is too much of it. I'm a big fan of Terry Pratchett's novels, but he nearly lost me in *Wee Free Men* with the Nac Mac Feegles dialect-ridden sentences. I was interested to note that later books in the same sequence included a glossary. Perhaps I wasn't alone?

When I was writing *Legends Walking* (also known as *Changer's Daughter*), I was in a quandary. Large segments of the book are set in Nigeria. Not only are multiple languages spoken in that one country, but the languages themselves are expressive of an entirely different way of thinking about concepts such as family relationships and even personal names. Moreover, there was no one accepted manner of transliteration. I eventually arrived at what I hoped was an acceptable compromise (and discussed some of the choices I had made in my Author's Note), but I was aware I had barely touched the complexity of those cultures.

Then there's the question of what to do with a named accent. In British novels, a type of accent will frequently be mentioned as "Cambridge" or "Yorkshire" or "Cockney." Sometimes the author puts the accent on the page as well. Other times, they do not. I remember reading about the Beatles having "Liverpool" (or sometimes "Liverpudlian") accents, but that didn't prepare me for the strange, flat, "holding the nose" manner in which they spoke the first time I heard a recorded interview.

I have heard young American readers of the Harry Potter novels admit to being surprised when they went to see the movies and Harry and his friends had British accents.

Jane Lindskold

Then there are all the American accents, some of which like "Southern" actually cover a wide range of accents. Others which, like "Maine" or "Bostonian," only apply to a very small region and a comparatively small segment of that region's population. How helpful are these designations to a reader not already familiar with the accent in question?

Sometime the author has a specific reason for phonetically writing out an accent. Terry Pratchett was using the Nac Mac Feegle's accent for humorous effect. Francis Hodgson Burnett in *The Secret Garden* makes learning to understand the Yorkshire dialect part of her characters' larger emotional journey.

A writer should also have a reason for weird punctuation, including accent marks and apostrophes. In her Pern novels, Anne McCaffery's dragonriders all have names that include apostrophes. However, there's a reason for this. Their "dragonrider names" are contractions of their birth names. The apostrophe isn't there to look "cool" or "Fantasy" or any such nonsense. It is there to indicate that a letter has been left out, just as the apostrophe in "don't" indicates that the second "o" in "do not" has been eliminated.

My gut feeling is that accents or peculiar spellings should be like seasoning. Employed with a light touch and understanding of their purpose and qualities, both have great value. Without this, they turn what could be an enjoyable experience into a distasteful one.

Wanderings on Writing

Getting to Know It...

You're writing a story. The characters are "live" and the plot is singing, but you realize that something's wrong, something's flat. After consideration, you realize that it's the setting.

Maybe you're writing a Fantasy set in a world that's sort of medieval. However, all you know about such worlds is what you've read in other Fantasy novels, or maybe from a role-playing game, or maybe a computer game... Of course, there was that section about the Middle Ages in your history class. And you do have a friend who was in the SCA. Still...

It's not enough. Where do you start learning more?

"Write about what you know" is a basic principle in most fiction writing courses. It's also one that most beginning SF/F writers rebel against. "I want to write about dragons! I want to write about wizards! Those don't exist except in fiction, so how can I 'know'? Can't I just make it up?"

Sure. But what are you going to make it up from? I hate to tell you this, but writing speculative fiction (an umbrella term that embraces Science Fiction, Fantasy, Horror, and their various offspring) isn't an excuse to do less research; it's a requirement to do more.

"What! How could I possibly need to do more? These things aren't real. I can do whatever I want!"

Not unless you want your readers to snarl at you. The "Twilight" novels have been very successful, but this hasn't kept lots of nasty comments from being made about Stephanie Meyers' unfamiliarity with the basics of folklore regarding vampires and werewolves. She has lots of readers, true, but she'd probably have even more if she hadn't shut out a large potential readership – and certainly she'd have spared herself a lot of grief.

"Well, can't I just sort of borrow from what other writers have done? I mean, they're my inspiration."

Yes. You can. I'll leave it to others to list the derivative authors who have been very successful. However, maintaining "voice" is very important to most writers. How can you have a voice if you're just copying someone else?

"Oh... All right. I'll at least think about doing some research."

Great! You'll be in good company. J.R.R. Tolkien did a lot of background work for his "Middle Earth." You can find some of it in *The Annals of Kings and Rulers* and other appendixes to *The Return of the King*. *The Silmarillion* is considered unreadable by many, but that's because it's not really a novel. My husband Jim (who is both a huge Tolkien fan and an anthropologist) said he suddenly understood the *The Simarillion* when he realized it was actually an origin story – an explanation for where everyone came from and of the roots of the current conflict – and not a novel.

I believe that one of the reasons that Tolkien's novels continue to garner new readers is because he was indeed writing about what he knew. He knew where his elves came from and his dwarves. He knew why various dragons lived in various places. He knew why there were balrogs. His novel might have been Fantasy, but he had worked out the foundations of his world.

"Does this mean I need to write hundreds of pages of foundation material before I ever start the novel?"

No. And, well, maybe, yes...

Let me give an example from my own work. *Through Wolf's Eyes* is, among other things, the story of the contest for the throne of Hawk Haven. First I had to work out why it was contested. "Simple," you say. "King Tedric doesn't have an heir and hasn't named one."

Wanderings on Writing

Simple? Hah! Questions of inheritance – especially when what is being inherited is a throne – are never simple. Look at the conflicts following the death of Henry VIII if you want a great example. Or watch the play (or marvelous film) *The Lion in Winter* (which is about King Henry II). Liberties were taken with the history, but it's a great demonstration of what happens when there are multiple potential heirs, each with strong claims.

But *Through Wolf's Eyes* isn't set in historical England. It's set in a fictional world. Therefore, first I had to ask myself who was eligible to inherit: The first born? Any child of the monarch? The favorite? The sister's son? (In some cultures, inheritance passes through the female line, even when females themselves aren't eligible.) Are females included?

I decided that, in Hawk Haven, inheritance would pass to the first born, females included, moving down the birth order in case of death.

However, in *Through Wolf's Eyes*, King Tedric's first born is dead. His second born is also dead (but her husband is around and some feel he has a claim). His third born is missing – and also disinherited. This would then move the possibilities sideways – to King Tedric's siblings and, because his siblings are fairly elderly, to their children.

I'm going to stop summarizing here. Suffice to say, before I could move into writing this stage of the novel, I had to design for myself the equivalent of a treatise on inheritance law in the Kingdom of Hawk Haven. I also had to write a complete family tree for King Tedric's family, going back several generations and forward to infant children.

To do this, I needed to compose biographical sketches of most of the people involved, explaining who they had married or why they had not married and if they had children. It took quite a bit of effort and a lot of going back and forth. However, when I was done, I had a solid foundation for the intrigues that underlay the action of the book.

Jane Lindskold

Now I was writing about what I *knew*. Much of what I knew didn't make it onto the page, any more than Tolkien introduced the history of Morgoth (who was responsible for the balrog) into *The Fellowship of the Ring*, but I *knew*.

And I could now write about what I know.

So You Want Dragons?

So... You want dragons. Despite the occasional reaction against dragons as overused – I have heard writers bragging that their Fantasy fiction is a "dragon-free zone" – I completely understand the impulse.

I've been visited by dragons in a few of my pieces. Of course, they were rather strange dragons... One was two-headed and rubber (Betwixt and Between from *Brother to Dragons, Companion to Owls*). Another was more an elemental spirit of treacherous nature than a fire-breathing lizard (the eponymous creature in *The Dragon of Despair*). Then there were the Chinese dragons featured in the "Breaking the Wall" novels. The fact that dragons are extinct is a major point in the athanor novels, *Changer* and *Legends Walking*.

That raises the first question. What sort of dragon do you want? Do you want something modeled on the classic European dragon? If you want this sort of dragon, do you want the simplest form – fire-breathing, violent, and destructive – or do you want the more refined model, still fire-breathing, still capable of violence, but also sophisticated, interested in riddle games and maybe even rulership?

Wanderings on Writing

Or are you looking for something closer to the Chinese dragon – or *lung* – a very different beast entirely? If you do your research, you'll find that there are several varieties of Chinese dragon, each associated with different landscapes, each with its own tastes and quirks. Which of these do you want?

Let's say you want something closer to the European dragon. Inspired by Smaug from *The Hobbit* (or perhaps the myths and legends that gave him birth), you want the more sophisticated model. You've decided that you'd like a male. He'll have scales of a burnished red, highlighted with copper. He flies, eats meat, hoards treasure, and demands the occasional virgin maiden.

Great! You're set!

Actually, not quite... A dragon of this sort is a peak predator – that is to say, at the top of the food chain. Even if he eats only occasionally (even lesser peak predators like wolves and great cats eat only a couple times a week), when he does, he eats a lot. Where is he getting this food? How do the locals feel about having their flocks – or game preserves – raided?

And that treasure... Where does he get it? Is it from forgotten days of yore or is he still building the collection? Why does he collect it? Long ago, I read an article in a gaming magazine that suggested the answer to this question was key to understanding the place of dragons in a given world. I have forgotten the source, but I still remember the question: "Do they just like lumpy beds?"

"Hey!" says the would-be writer of speculative fiction. "Does this really matter? I just want the dragon so my hero has something to go after, a quest, y'know, maybe an initiation challenge."

Well, sure, if you want your novel to have the depth and lasting power of this year's current hot computer game, that's enough. Kill the dragon and level-up. There's satisfaction in that. I've played those games and felt it. But we're talking about writing a story here, maybe even one that will have some staying power in the reader's imagination when "World of the Wyrm" is forgotten by all but die-hard gamers.

Let's look at Smaug... Smaug's treasure was what brought the dwarves (and Bilbo) to him; most were after wealth, but a few of the more senior dwarves knew that things of great power were hidden there.

Smaug didn't emerge from his lair very often, but when he did the people of Laketown suffered. That meant they were both willing to fight against Smaug and – in the latter part of the story – felt they had a right to some of the loot, enough of a right that they were willing to go to war to secure their share. Their neighbors also had a long relationship with Smaug. Even those who had not been victims of the dragon's greed and rapine knew about the treasure – and wanted it.

These same questions underlie the action in an SF treatment of dragons. In *Dragonflight*, the first book of Anne McCaffery's Pern novels, the locals are getting tired of supporting the "useless" dragons in the Weyrs. They also don't approve of what they see as essentially sacrificing a virgin or two. By underpinning her science fictional concept with these mythic resonances, Mc-Caffery gives her piece depth. Her twist that the big, fire-breathing, peak predators (who do, in fact, have a "taste" for virgins) are ultimately not monsters but saviors, reshaped the concept of the dragon in both Science Fiction and Fantasy.

Dealing with Dragons by Patricia Wrede provides a creative answer to the question of why dragons demand human princesses. I don't want to offer a spoiler so I'll settle for saying that this book – and its sequels – don't just provide a twist. They use the twist as a fascinating foundation for a new setting.

Teeth and Claw by Jo Walton is another novel that takes the politics of intelligent dragons to a new level. Initially, the dragons could be humans with, well, teeth and claws. Then, just as the reader gets comfortable with this, Walton shows you that her characters are not human at all. Then the book becomes truly draconic.

So, why think about your dragons? Your pegasi? Your unicorns? Isn't it a lot of work for nothing? (I mean, everyone knows what a dragon is.) I hope the examples above give you an idea why you might bother and why bothering not only makes for a better story, it also can be creatively stimulating and (dare I say it?) just plain fun!

Living and Growing With Characters

Series are very popular but what is expected of a series has changed. Not long ago, the characters in a series could remain essentially static. Although the examples that spring most quickly to my mind are from Mystery novels – Hercule Poroit, Miss Marple, Spenser – there were plenty in SF/F as well.

These days, there is a greater demand for characters that evolve, and that character evolution puts demands on the writer.

I've written several series: the two athanor books (*Changer* and *Legends Walking*), the six Firekeeper books (starting with *Through Wolf's Eyes* and going through *Wolf's Blood*), and the three "Breaking the Wall" books (*Thirteen Orphans*, *Nine Gates*, and *Five Odd Honors*), and now the newly launched "Artemis Awakening" series.

In addition, I've done series short stories: my three Captain Allie stories (now available as an e-book under the title *Star Messenger*), my three "Andrasta" stories, at least four stories featuring the Albuquerque Adepts, a couple featuring Lillianara and the android, Alastar, and a couple featuring a Chinese mage named Tieh. (If you want publication information on any of these, go to my website, www.janelindskold.com; they'll be listed under Other Works).

I've also done three series stories set in David Weber's "Honorverse." "Queen's Gambit" tells how the current reigning queen of Manticore took the throne. "Promised Land" and "Ruthless" focus more on Elizabeth's younger brother, Michael. Weber and I wrote two novels about Stephanie Harrington, *Fire Season* and *Treecat Wars*.

The reason that I like writing series stories is that because, once you've created the background, a lot of the setting is in place. This leaves more mental room to focus on characters and plot.

Let me use the stories in *Star Messenger* as an example. I created Captain "Allie" Ah-Lee for a story called "Winner Takes Trouble" for the anthology *Alien Pets*. She's a singleship captain, strong and independent, the sort of character I enjoyed reading about in the works of such writers as Larry Niven, Andre Norton, Clifford Simak, and Poul Anderson.

Allie begins these stories as an adult with a profession, a spaceship of her own, and a lot of life history. That made her fun to write about because she has a history that I got to share with the reader.

In "Winner Takes Trouble," Allie wins an alien creature in a poker game. When, a few years later, I was invited to write a story for an anthology called *Guardsmen of Tomorrow*, I immediately thought, "Hey, this would be a great opportunity to explore Allie's background." Allie likes to bend rules, so casting her as a "guard" of any sort was a fun challenge. A story called "Endpoint Insurance" resulted.

Wanderings on Writing

Later still, I was asked to contribute to the anthology, *You Bet Your Planet*. In "Winner Takes Trouble," Allie had already been established as a gambler. In "Here To There," she takes on her biggest gamble ever – one where she's the only person playing who realizes that the peaceful coexistence of several races may be decided by who wins a "reality show" type game.

There's a special challenge to writing a series character who begins the series relatively young. Especially if the books span a good number of years, the character needs to grow and change a great deal while, at the same time, remaining recognizable as the person whom the reader started out with.

My most long-running series, both in terms of books and in terms of the years of the characters' lives, are my Firekeeper books. In *Through Wolf's Eyes*, Firekeeper is about fifteen years old. For as long as she can remember, she has lived with wolves, as a wolf. Only in her dreams does she remember anything about her life as a human. Writing from Firekeeper's point of view at this early stage in the series was very challenging. Although she has language, she has no reference points for anything to do with human culture, including such basics as clothing and domestic animals. I basically had to create an alternate vocabulary for her, one that would make sense without driving the reader (and myself) nuts.

As the series progressed and Firekeeper acquired a familiarity with human customs, the challenge was to keep her recognizably "other" without making her stagnant. I handled this by having Firekeeper – no matter how much she learned about human culture – persist in thinking of herself as an oddly-shaped wolf. This manner of thinking provided a well-balanced – if decidedly peculiar – person. Firekeeper's companion, the wolf Blind Seer, often quotes from wolf proverbs to provide a sense of wolf culture. In fact, he does this so often that Firekeeper starts accusing him of making them up!

Firekeeper is the youngest of the point-of-view characters, but several of the others are comparatively young. Derian and Elise begin the books in their late teens. By the end of the series, both have experienced a great deal. From people with unfocused dreams, they become people with responsibilities – responsibilities they have chosen based on their varied experiences. In their own ways, they were as complicated to develop as the more obviously alien Firekeeper.

A related challenge is writing a series where one or more of the characters are quite young children. In the "Breaking the Wall" series, Nissa Nita has a two-and-a-half year-old daughter named 'Lani. When a child is that young, even a month can mean significant differences in interests and abilities. Birthdays are a big deal, for parent as well as for child. Even though 'Lani is a comparatively minor character, I had to keep track of the passage of time and adapt her accordingly.

I've never been fond of series where characters don't change at all, although I will make exceptions. I like both Agatha Christie's Hercule Poroit and Miss Marple. I can accept that they don't change much because, from their first appearance forward, both are quite elderly. The skills that they need to draw upon to be successful in their chosen lives are ones they already possess in great quantity. Why should they change?

It's important to note that Christie could and did write characters who changed. Her recurring characters Tommy and Tuppence (first appearance, *The Secret Adversary*) change a great deal over the years from their first appearance as young people, recently "demobbed" from service in World War I, through later books where they are married and have children of their own.

Christie showed that an older person may change a great deal if the right stimulus is applied. Mr. Sattherwaite, the point-of-view character for the stories collected in *The Mysterious Mr. Quinn*, begins as an older man, set in his ways, believing – and even content – that life has passed him by. By the end of the series, he has been changed by his experiences and has become a player in the game of life, rather than merely an observer.

Wanderings on Writing

Something I like even less than characters who don't change at all are those who change in either the direction of near perfection or of being so shattered by their experiences that they are jittering balls of nerves and quirks. Both strike me as variations on lazy characterization. The first is dull and – especially in Science Fiction and Fantasy – can verge on turning the characters into superheroes. The second ignores that, even when people are hit hard by adversity, they usually acquire some interesting coping mechanisms.

So, when you start your series, remember change applies to more than plot. It applies to characters as well.

Victims and Villains

A while back, the *Magic and Mayhem* site asked me to write about victims or villains in my fiction. I was rather shocked, since I didn't think I wrote either. I'm actually rather passionate about the subject. The following piece is what I gave them instead.

I try not to write either victims or villains. When talking about the characters in my books, I don't even use the words "heroes" and "villains." Protagonists and antagonists, sure, but not villains and never victims.

Yes. Some characters in my books become victims within the unfolding of events. Perhaps the character I've been given the most grief over is Citrine. I will admit that in the course of the "Wolf Series" (also known as the "Firekeeper Saga"), Citrine goes through a really bad patch.

Jane Lindskold

As for villains, I'm a firm believer that no one, not even historical figures – like Stalin or Hitler, who were responsible for the deaths and torture of many millions of people – gets up in the morning, rubs his or her hands briskly together, and says, to paraphrase S.M. Stirling, : "Ah-hah! I think I'll do something really evil today."

For this reason, in my novels, you're not going to find any glowing eye in the sky brooding over a devastated landscape. If characters dress all in black with skulls for jewelry, they're into Goth fashion. What you will find in my novels are people who commit completely heinous acts (like having their own child's finger chopped off) and yet still manage to believe that what they are doing is all for the greater good.

Yes. I do believe in evil, but I also believe in the capacity of intelligent beings of any type to justify their actions so they come out as the "good guys." Read interviews with serial killers. Most see *themselves* as the victims. The same goes for leaders of genocidal armies, instigators of mass suicides, or even professional torturers. It's all the other guy's fault or, at creepy best, a bit of fun that got out of control.

I've never been one of those writers – and I know some who do this – who deliberately create a character to serve as a victim in order to manipulate reader reaction. I've heard writers brag about doing this: creating the cute kid or kitten or whatever that is meant to die and so bring tears to the reader's eyes. When I hear this sort of discussion, I have to dig my nails into the palm of my hand and force a polite nod. I really despise such deliberate manipulation as sloppy writing and abuse of the reader.

If a character in one of my books is harmed, I feel it. I'm not ashamed to admit that I've wept for these fictional people. When I had to write the scene where Changer loses his eye – a scene that had to be "on-stage" – I wrote around it until I could get up the courage.

Wanderings on Writing

So, victims and villains. You'll find them both in my works, but I never think of them as such. To me, they're all people, doing what they do because that's how the world has worked out for them.

Note: A version of this piece originally appeared on the blog site *Magic and Mayhem* in March of 2010.

Dystopias and Anti-Heroes

This weekend, as Jim and I were cutting up vegetables for curry, we ended up talking about dystopias and anti-heroes.

Seriously... We really did. This is NOT just an excuse for a topic.

Anyhow, Jim was saying that he didn't much like fiction set in dystopias. Knowing something about both his reading and viewing preferences, I told him I didn't think this was actually the case. I pointed out that lots of very good stories take place in dystopian settings. A dystopia is simply a fictional setting which is diseased or corrupt either politically or environmentally (or sometimes both). Such settings are often very good for fiction because the protagonists have a lot of challenges to work against.

During the Cold War, these dystopias were often under the control of totalitarian governments that pretended to be promoting some ostensibly positive philosophy (usually a variation on socialism or communism), but were really creating a tiered society in which those on top lived a lot better than the bulk of the population.

Jane Lindskold

These days, environmental catastrophes (rather than an abstract political philosophy) have become the reason for the dominating regime to become established. The world is in trouble. Extreme control is needed. The mass of the population is subjected to severe, even harsh, restrictions. As with the earlier incarnations, there is usually a segment of the population who is living very well – in direct contrast to the policies they enforce.

In both these earlier and later trends of fictional dystopias, the government may be a theocracy of some sort. (Although sometimes the "god" is a leader, since Marxist philosophy speaks out against organized religion.) After all, what better way to maintain control than to have the divine on your side?

Jim and I started discussing books and movies we'd both enjoyed that used dystopian settings. I mentioned Heinlein's various "Crazy Years" stories. Jim brought up the movies *Rollerball* and *Blade Runner*. I mentioned Pratchett's *Small Gods*. Jim mentioned Zelazny's *Lord of Light*. From there we went on to a lot of the cyberpunk material. In the end, we both agreed that it wasn't the dystopian settings we disliked, but the frequent cases where dystopias seemed to become an excuse for authors to create whining, unattractive, and simply just plain annoying and/or ineffectual characters whom we're supposed to accept (or at least pity) because they are against (or oppressed by) the dystopian regime.

For this reason, neither of us much cared for Orwell's classics *1984* or *Animal Farm*. Or Huxley's *Brave New World*.

This led us to anti-heroes. Anti-heroes are a more difficult concept to define than dystopia because the question of what is heroic and what is not heroic shifts with both the time period and the culture. Even the definitions of the term vary from source to source. (Take a look on-line if you're curious). Some definitions say that the anti-hero has "no" heroic qualities. Others say that anti-heroes are lacking in some heroic qualities, while possessing others.

55

Wanderings on Writing

If I were to take a stab at a definition, I would say that an anti-hero behaves in a recognizably heroic fashion in some sense, but does not embrace the idealized concept of how a hero should behave.

What do I mean by behaving in a "recognizably heroic fashion in some sense"? Usually, the anti-hero is on the side of what would be recognized as "good." He might be a bit of a bully, but he's *our* bully, fighting worse bullies. She might be a vigilante (therefore, outside of the law), but the people she's taking down are operating in a fashion so that the law cannot or (as is often the case in a dystopia) will not touch them.

As for the idealized concept of how a hero might behave... Its evolution is so complex that I can't possibly cover it all here. However, one of the major influences on the modern concept of the hero in "Western" civilization was the medieval courtly and chivalric romances. These included the concepts of a fair fight, treating a lady with courtesy, and honoring your ruler (and often his legal code).

While serving as a fine, civilizing influence, these chivalric romances were not in the least practical, nor were their ideals followed in "real life." Nevertheless, the concept is so attractive that it keeps cropping up. You find an updated version in many Westerns (novels, television shows, and movies), where the "white hat" hero won't shoot to kill, is more likely to kiss his horse than the girl, and does his good deed, then rides off into the sunset without asking for reward – or even thanks.

Early Science Fiction, especially space operas – which were often Westerns translated into outer space, rather than being set on a more or less historical frontier – also adopted these ideas.

As I said above, the concept of heroic behavior changes with time periods and cultures. The Greek hero Theseus was considered a great hero at the time his stories originated, but I doubt that someone who builds his reputation by brawling, murdering, and stealing, then abandons the girl who gave up everything to help him, would be considered a hero today. John Gardner's novel *Grendel* retold the Beowulf saga from the monster's point of view – and showed the burly hero in a much more unattractive light than he would have been seen by the culture which created him.

Robin Hood is a great example of how the reasons behind actions, rather than the actions themselves, make the difference between an anti-hero and a villain. If Robin Hood had robbed from the rich to line his pockets, he would have been a villain. However, because he robs from the rich to give to the poor and flouts the law to correct its abuses, he is an anti-hero. The classic film with Errol Flynn shows this perfectly. Maid Marian's view of the dashing rogue doesn't change because he is charming and has a brilliant smile, but because she sees what he does for others.

I think one reason we like anti-heroes is that they are more believable than idealized heroes. As much as we love the Lone Ranger (classic version), it's hard to believe that we'd be able to shoot to wound when being rushed by a dozen furious outlaws, all armed to the teeth. Arthurian legend shows how vulnerable a hero becomes when an impersonal code replaces personal justice.

Yet, as appealing as anti-heroes can be, writing them well is a dangerous balancing act. It's far too easy for an anti-hero to slip over the line into villainy. Carrie Vaughn dealt with this challenge beautifully in her "Kitty" books. The vampire hunter Cormac steps over the line and goes to jail for it – this despite the fact that he is an appealing character, one who helped Kitty a great deal in her adjustment to the supernatural world. I'm sure I'm not the only reader who expected to pick up the book following Cormac's arrest to find that he'd escaped or gotten off on a technicality. It was refreshing to find a story where, when the anti-hero steps over the line into villainy, he pays the price.

As with anything where "grey" rather than "black" and "white" rule, both dystopias and anti-heroes can be more difficult to write than their more clean-cut counterparts, but the reward is well worth the effort.

Writing the Villain

As I explained in "Victims and Villains" earlier, when I'm writing, I don't think of any character as a villain. The following piece developed from an on-line discussion in which the word was already actively being used. I've decided to preserve it here because, sometimes, it's good to think about the antagonist in the light of the traditional villain!

A complex, convincing villain can make or break a book. Having that villain's point of view is also important, especially in a certain type of story.

Just because I want to make sure we're talking about the same thing, let me define a couple of terms, okay?

It's quite possible to define villains without using abstractions like "evil" and by focusing on specific qualities. Villains care more about their own gain than what will happen to anyone else around them. They do serious harm, not to be "evil," but because the end result will benefit themselves. Villains have allies and associates, but rarely friends (because a friend is someone whose benefit or happiness is important). Even when his or her acts may seem virtuous, a villain's acts ultimately benefit the doer, not those ostensibly done for.

An antagonist is somewhat different from a villain. If the protagonist is the character who represents the main thrust of the action in the book, the antagonist is the character who opposes those actions. An antagonist may not be nearly as nasty as a villain. He or she (or they) may have many admirable qualities and just be on the "wrong" side. In fact, if the author lets the reader into the antagonist's head and shares something of the antagonist's motivations, the question of who is the "good guy" can become a matter of point of view.

I know I write good villains. If I didn't, I wouldn't get e-mails from readers yelling at me for doing such horrible things to my characters. One memorable e-mail informed me that I couldn't put off onto Lady Melina from "The Firekeeper Saga" what she did to young Citrine because I created Melina and so it was I who had done it...

Wow! By that logic, I also eat raw rabbit guts and walk around in public without my clothes on, as my "heroic" (or at least anti-heroic) Firekeeper does.

However, this leads nicely to the first trick to writing good villains. Accept that, although various people are going to wonder how you manage to come up with such twisted and ugly material, the characters who perform those acts are not you. You'll have to realize that some readers are going to wonder just what perversities you practice in your spare time, but letting the dark side out is part of the cost of being a writer.

(Aside: Some of the nicest people I've met write Horror. Ellen Datlow, one of the finest editors in the Horror field, is an intelligent and eloquent lady. Maybe there's something to be said for coming to terms with the Dark.)

Another element in writing good villains is accepting that *they* don't think they're villains. In their version of the story, they're – if not heroes – simply people with the good sense to do what is necessary to achieve their goals. As Steve (S.M.) Stirling frequently puts it: "No one wakes up in the morning and says 'I think I'm going to be evil today.'" Even Hitler convinced himself he was doing what he was doing for the greater good.

Wanderings on Writing

Recently, Jim and I re-watched a bunch of classic animated Disney movies. To me, the reason the Lady Tremaine in *Cinderella* is so much more terrifying than Malificent in *Sleeping Beauty* is because Lady Tremaine is intelligently malicious when pursuing those actions that serve her goals. (In this case, promoting the welfare of her two daughters over that of her stepdaughter.) Malificent, by contrast, lightly talks of "evil" and uses a minor social slight as an excuse to pursue this nebulous abstract. She may turn into a dragon and have orc-like henchmen, but she's much less frightening.

(Aside: It's particularly interesting to contrast these two characters because they were voiced by the same actress. She also provided the physical type upon which both were modeled.)

Happily, we're not likely to meet a Malificent in our lives. I find myself terrified of Lady Tremaine because I've already met variations on her – and am likely to do so again. Because this is the type of villain who scares me, it's also the type I write, even if I find immersing myself into that point of view highly distasteful.

There's a scene in my novel *Changer* in which the Changer has an eye extracted while he is awake and completely conscious of what is going on. That scene had to be in the book and from his point of view. I hated writing it – I wrote around it for as long as possible – but in the end, I dove in. In *Five Odd Honors*, the third "Breaking the Wall" book, young Flying Claw is methodically tortured. Again, I hated writing this scene, but it had to be there. To write it well, I had to go into the twisted insanity of those for whom this was a sensible and reasonable approach to achieving their goals. I had to get across that, to them, Flying Claw was the unreasonable one.

Scary stuff.

So why write from the villain's point of view or with an understanding of why they do what they do? Why go into those places? Isn't the end result enough?

Jane Lindskold

Once upon a time, I thought this was the case. I enjoy classic Mystery novels. In those, you rarely know who did the murder or why the murder was done until the end of the book. When I wrote my first several published novels – the first two of which were from a first-person point of view – the Mystery approach was my model.

After my second novel, *Marks of Our Brothers*, came out, author Mike (Michael A.) Stackpole said to me something along these lines: "I liked it, but I think it would have been stronger if you also provided something of the other side's point of view."

My initial reaction was to disagree. The novel was told from a first-person point of view. How could I introduce someone else's without that introduction seeming forced? Also – thinking about those Mysteries again – wouldn't knowing what "the bad guys" were up to "give away" the plot?

Since then, I've come to understand what Mike was saying. I've noticed how tense I get when I read a novel that provides what the "bad guys" are thinking and planning. David Weber is very good at using this technique. I remember being on the edge of my seat as I read an Honor Harrington novel wherein we the readers knew that the enemy had developed a new surveillance technology that invalidated a bunch of the tactics that Honor and her associates were going to use. How many ships would be destroyed, how many lives lost, before they discovered this and took countermeasures?

Would I write *Marks of Our Brothers* differently today? Probably so.

You don't need to make a villain a point-of-view character to use their perspective effectively. What's important is making certain that the reader understands that the villain thinks of himself or herself as following a reasonable, intelligent, and sensible course of action. However, sometimes, presenting how the other side thinks is valuable, even compelling.

Wanderings on Writing

Find Out What You Know

Shall I admit it? I like detail. Okay... Let me rephrase that. I like certain kinds of detail. I am immune to the charm of entering long lines of computer code. Tax forms give me hives and palpitations.

When I say I like detail, what I mean is I love knowing what underlies the familiar. If you've ever read the Thursday Tangents, one of the weekly features of my blog, you've probably figured this out. My collaborator, Alan Robson, is more patient than you know about my myriad questions. Of course, he gets in a few of his own, now and then.

I really get excited by how ideas fit together, as anyone knows who has had the misfortune to be in the vicinity when I have a new obsession. Then I will happily prattle on about whatever has just caught my fancy. This interest in detail is really not a bad trait for a writer of Fantasy and Science Fiction, since these are genres in which knowing where things come from can save a writer from making embarrassing errors.

So how do you start learning about something about which you know nothing? Do you need to sign up for a course at the local college or prowl the web? No. Nothing so complex. The former is time-consuming and the latter demands a real skill in assessing your sources for validity.

A fun-and-easy way to give yourself a foundation in anything from a historical period to fashions in clothing to industrial processes to wildlife biology – well, to just about anything except tax forms and computer programming – is to read the simple books written for children between the ages of about eight and eleven.

Let me give an example. When I was writing the Firekeeper books, I wanted to have the economy of New Kelvin be based on being able to supply a commodity not available anywhere else. I decided to settle on silk. Why? I like silk.

However, despite the fact that I like silk, all I knew about how it was produced was that it came from what was usually called a silkworm. From reading the excellent novel *Bridge of Birds* by Barry Hughart, I knew these weren't worms of the sort I dig up in my garden, but more like caterpillars. Clearly, if I was going to base an export economy on silk, I needed to know more.

Surely, you say, sericulture (that's the cultivation of silkworms) is not something you'll find covered in children's books. Guess what? It is! Even in our relatively small local library system, I found several that covered the subject. I took these home.

From their pages, I acquainted myself with all sorts of interesting facts. For example, an adult silkworm moth has a wingspan of about two inches. It reproduces sexually. Adult life span is brief – a few days or weeks. I learned that a silkworm's cocoon is made from a single unbroken thread more than a mile long. Sericulturalists heat-kill the moths to keep them from breaking the cocoon when they emerge. And, yep, to get the thread, the cocoons need to be unwound – again, without breaking that thread.

From this start I went on. I learned that, although the silkworm that produces the silk you'll find in your local clothing store is of one particular type, there are related insects that produce a similar thread. These can be found in different climates and not all of them require mulberry leaves...

Wanderings on Writing

Whoa! There I go again... Still, how many of you have some beauty in your Fantasy novel wearing a silk gown? Does she live in a land of ice and cold, the type of climate where silkworms could never thrive? I guess there's a good trade route available. There isn't? Then where does she get her silk? Maybe giant spiders? Who raises them? What do they eat?

It's all interconnected...

One of the great things about children's books as sources is that, since they're written for young people, nothing is assumed. Words are defined. Often the definitions are repeated in a simple glossary. Another great thing is that there are many pictures, not only photographs, but often drawings, including cut-away diagrams that show you how things work.

Those pictures and glossaries can be a gem beyond price. Armed with the knowledge you can garner from them, you're prepared to move ahead. Maybe you'll move to texts written for older children. Maybe you'll jump all the way to texts written for adults. Maybe now you'll be able to tackle that interesting website that was so confusing the first time.

Or maybe you'll realize that you have enough to get you going with that part of your story which you didn't feel was coming out quite right.

I love detail. I realize that not everyone thinks that reading a book about the evolution of fabric-making techniques is fun. I do, and did. And now I know where to go if I want to figure out just how velvet is made...

Jane Lindskold

How Much is Too Much?

One of the things I do to recharge my writerly batteries is read non-fiction. One of the books I read during one such session is the lushly gorgeous *Horses: Myth and Fascination* by Susanne Sgrazzutti. The book has several sections, one of which is devoted entirely to the complicated and sometimes confusing terminology associated with horse coloration and markings.

I first encountered many of these terms in Marguerite Henry's *All About Horses*, a book that was given to me when I was ten or twelve and which still has an honored place on my bookshelf. At the start of Chapter 13 the author says:

> *"If we are riding across country and meet an old friend on a new horse, how nice to be able to say, 'What a beautiful buckskin (or sorrel, or flea-bitten gray)!'*
>
> *"Or if we're at the races, watching the entries parade to the post, how nice to be able to say, 'I like the chestnut first, then the sandy bay.'"*

Well, of course, I agreed with Ms. Henry. I wanted to know what made one horse a "chestnut" and another merely "brown." Why was that horse a buckskin but this other one – so close in coloration – a dun? Why was one face marking a "blaze" and another a "stripe"? At what point did a stocking become a sock? Ms. Henry elucidated these mysteries and many others.

Wanderings on Writing

Later, I learned that terms for coloration varied according to region and culture as well. Terms commonly used in American horse circles such as "pinto" and "palomino" come to us through the Spanish who contributed so much to the language of the American West and to American English in general. I remember being vaguely puzzled when, in one of Susan Cooper's novels, someone is described as riding a "lion-colored" horse. When I sorted through the description, I realized that what she meant was a palomino.

Ms. Sgrazzutti's book provides yet another angle on this mystery. Her book was originally written in German and traces of the German terminology creep over. One example is when she refers to what an American would call an "Arabian" as an "Arabian Thoroughbred." To most American horse fanciers, a "Thoroughbred" is a specific type of race horse. As Ms. Henry says: "to a horseman a Thoroughbred is always a horse whose ancestry can be traced directly to the Byerly Turk, Darley's Arabian, or the Godolphin Arabian."

Even more fun was discovering that the German color system was designed by one man – Eduard Meyer – in the 1930's. For this reason, a grey horse is mold-colored, while one with a wildly-spotted coat is referred to as a "Tigerschecke" or "spotted tiger."

Now, when I say this is "fun," I suppose I should clarify. I find this a tremendous amount of fun because I find horses beautiful and interesting. Therefore, I find the language associated with them interesting. I must admit, I would not feel at all the same about, say, guns. I quite enjoy Mysteries and Thrillers, but when the writers pause to lovingly describe a certain model of gun for no other reason than that they want to, I get frustrated. (I feel differently if the distinctions have some value to the plot.)

I am fond of Steve (S.M.) Stirling's "Change" books, but sometimes I feel as if I should have my dictionary of armor by my side when he starts describing what his characters are wearing. All those technical terms for types of helmets and breastplates and the like mean less than nothing to me. They actually make what his characters are wearing less clear than if he stuck to less accurate, more general terms.

Too technical a definition becomes worse than no description at all. Why? Because a description that relies on too specific a vocabulary may be the equivalent of saying "gobble-wibble wibble-wobble." Don't believe me? Let's try an example.

I bet most of you would have no problem following me if I described a horse as having a "star." You'd even position it correctly on the horse in question. However, would you understand what the difference was if I said the horse had a "flower"? Without context, would you even know where the flower was, or that it was a marking, not an ornament? Possibly not. Why? Because the term "star" as a marking on a horse has entered common usage. It's dramatic to describe the hero riding into town on his black horse with the star on its brow. Less so if he rides in on a black horse with a flower…

But both are legitimate terms for equine markings that mean subtly different things to a horse fancier. (A star is more angular, a flower more a rounded blotch. A flake, by the by, is a very small blotch. All are located on the face. If elsewhere, other terms are used.)

How about "overo piebald" or "tobiano skewbald"?

A careful writer can combine accurate use of any sort of terminology by melding it with description, but this needs to be carefully handled. Take a look at the subtle differences between these descriptions.

"Marshall Kane rode out to confront the bandits on his chestnut gelding with the white stripe."

"Marshall Kane rode out to confront the bandits on his ruddy chestnut gelding with the white stripe down its nose."

Wanderings on Writing

"Marshall Kane rode out to confront the bandits on Flame, his chestnut gelding with the white stripe down its nose."

The first is perfectly accurate and would tell someone who knew horses that the horse was reddish brown and had a thin white stripe on its nose. However, someone who didn't know horses might envision a horse with zebra markings or a lightning bolt on its flank. "Chestnut" is descriptive – if you know what a chestnut is. If you don't, it doesn't immediately conjure "reddish brown."

The second description bridges the gap between accurate terminology and description. The third uses the horse's name "Flame" to hint at the coloration.

Which would I use? Honestly, I'd probably skip the term "stripe" (which describes a narrow white line; a marking, just to confuse matters further, that is also called a "race") entirely and go for the more familiar "blaze." I'd hazard "chestnut," but find a way to slip in "reddish brown" when possible. "Dismounting, he placed a hand on the horse's reddish brown shoulder."

Let's dance back to those German terms for a moment. What if I had a German character? Shouldn't I use German terminology? Well, it could be colorful. (I have a mad desire to have some character ride a spotted tiger in some future book.) However, would it add interesting world-building or merely confuse my reader? How much is great fun and how much is too much? Whether describing horses or guns or types of food or whatever fascinates you, that's something writers need to consider.

Jane Lindskold

Facts or Fiction

A while back, fellow author Paul Genesse sent me a nice long e-mail talking about my novel, *The Buried Pyramid*. He complimented me for my use of Egyptian material, both historical and mythological, noting that although he is an avowed "Egyptophile" I had included some elements he had never seen used in that fashion before.

Well, of course, I was tickled. Paul's comments got me thinking about writing historical fiction in general and in particular the question of just how historically accurate can one make the material without alienating the readers.

When I was writing *The Buried Pyramid*, I researched my material on several levels. My novel is set in the 1870's, so first I needed to make myself familiar with that time period. I'll just give one example of the complexities.

This turned out to be a period of transition in women's fashions. Unlike today, older generations often held onto the styles of their "day" while the younger people were more adventurous. Therefore, I needed to be familiar with both older and cutting edge fashions.

I remember my copy editor querying me about the point where Jenny goes to the bazaar wearing a "daring" ankle-length gown. The copy editor asked if I meant something shorter. However, at that time, especially for a young lady of good reputation, an ankle-length skirt was very, very daring, just like Jenny herself.

The Buried Pyramid offered me challenges far beyond fashion. As I noted, most of the book is set in the 1870's. However, there's a point where things get very, very weird. For that section, I needed the most up-to-date information available about ancient Egypt. Therefore, I had to divide my Egypt research into two parts: one

Wanderings on Writing

for the Egypt my characters would know and one for an ancient Egypt as close to "real" as I could get.

Happily, I have a friend who shares my enthusiasm for matters of Egyptian history. He loaned me a bunch of books, including travel journals written by people who were in Egypt at the same time my characters were. I had a wonderful time immersing myself in the material. I even learned some elementary hieroglyphs and their varied meanings. Fun!

One problem with about writing historical fiction is that some historical realities are distinctly unpleasant. Here I'm not talking about the things everyone brings up, like body odor or the prevalence of disease. I'm talking about social attitudes.

One of my favorite examples of this is illustrated by the attitude shown towards a couple of social customs in two popular Roman Mystery series: the "Novels of Ancient Rome" written by Steven Saylor and the SPQR Mysteries written by John Maddox Roberts. These books are set in roughly the same time period. In a couple of cases, the action even centers around the same events. However, in my opinion, Roberts does a far better job of getting into the mindset of a Roman of that time period.

Saylor's main character is uncomfortable with slavery. He frees a slave and – if I recall correctly – even marries her. He's basically a twentieth-century American in a toga.

Roberts' character Decius is completely comfortable with slavery. He keeps slaves and is unsentimental about them. When Decius sets up housekeeping on his own, his family gives him a couple of elderly retainers, much as today parents might give their kids the old furniture from the storage unit. Decius is happy to have these slaves – even if he wishes he could have younger slaves, and, especially, slaves who didn't know him from the time he was a child and so feel free to nag.

Admittedly, Decius is something of an eccentric. He actually cares "who dunnit" and why, whereas his family is mostly interested in what political advantage can be gained from murders and other scandalous events. However, except for this, he is very much a man of his time.

Decius is young and lusty, quite capable (especially in the earlier books) of getting into affairs that aren't exactly wise. However, when the time comes for him to marry, Decius is not led by either his heart or his desires. He knows that, for a Roman, marriage is a means of social advancement and of cementing ties for his family with other families. He's lucky that one girl among those who are suggested as suitable – the niece of a rising politician named Gaius Julius Caesar – is also quite to his liking.

No marriages to slaves for him!

Later on in the series, Decius does free his body slave, a young man named Hermes, but not out of any sentiment that slavery is wrong or that Hermes "deserves" to be free. Decius simply decides that it would be advantageous to him to have Hermes be able to function as a freedman, since slaves were barred from certain areas.

Demonstrating the responsibility of Roman slaveholder to house slave, Decius waits until the somewhat impulsive young Hermes is ready for the responsibility of freedom. He also comforts himself with the awareness that legally Hermes will remain his client, bound to him within the complex rules that govern client-patron relationship. Thus, Decius will not lose a valuable associate, nor will Hermes be out of a job.

So when writing a novel set in a historical time period, it's not enough to research the clothing and weapons. It's important to consider the social attitudes as well. Otherwise, you're not really writing historical fiction. You're writing the literary equivalent of a costume ball.

Wanderings on Writing

Awkward Realities

In the essay "Facts or Fiction," I talked about some of the challenges – and interesting things – one encounters when writing about a long-ago historical period. What is not as often discussed is how time periods closer to our own can blindside a writer.

Lately, I've been reading a lot of fiction that would have been considered roughly "contemporary" when I was younger (and I'm not *that* old), but is now showing how quickly social attitudes can change. One good example comes from the works of Australian writer Arthur Upfield.

While reading these excellent novels, I was reminded how casually acceptable racism was only a few generations ago. Upfield chose to model his detective – Napoleon Bonaparte – after a half-aboriginal, half-white friend of his called Tracker Leon. With such a character, racial issues were going to be in the forefront of any story.

However, little elements showed that this casual racial stereotyping went far beyond the black (as the aboriginals are called) versus white divide. In *The Lure of the Bush*, a man who has just found an interesting trail is described as "walking in small circles with the earnest downward scrutiny of a Scotsman looking for a lost sixpence." Today that would be flagged as "negative stereotyping."

Coincidentally, I've been listening to a bunch of novels by Agatha Christie. (Audio books are my favorite way of making doing chores amusing.) Many of these are from the same general time period as Upfield's work.

From these you can see that, even in "civilized" England, casual racism was rampant. Mind you, Christie often demonstrates how short-sighted these views are, but the fact that Hercule Poroit – despite his credentials – is often dismissed as foolish simply because he is a "foreigner" shows how prevalent such ideas were. Captain Hastings, Poroit's good friend, is not immune to such short-sightedness. To him, his admired associate is the exception to the accepted rule.

Upfield also demonstrated how our attitude toward animals has changed in the last few decades. In *The Lure of the Bush*, a young man who is meant to be quite admirable rides a horse to death, stalks a large cod with the intent of spearing it, and beats a dingo to death with his stirrup iron. Today, such behavior would be a quick and easy way to characterize the man as, if not precisely a villain, certainly a brute.

Another time, another place, you say, but such differences in attitude can trip up a writer who thinks that people even a short time ago are just like we are today.

Consider social habits. A while back, an on-line review site focused on Roger Zelazny's ten-volume *Chronicles of Amber*. In the article, the reviewer commented about how frequently the characters smoked. I was amused, since the topic had come up when Roger and I were corresponding. I later touched upon why Roger's characters were invariably smokers in the biography I wrote.

Roger said: "My characters smoked in most of my early stories because whenever I was momentarily stuck in the course of a narrative I would light a cigarette. My usual reaction was then to transfer it. 'Of course,' I would think. 'He lit a cigarette.'" (letter, 29 May 1989)

That comment came back to me last week when I was reading *The Day of the Triffids* by John Wyndham. The main character smokes a lot – and so does his girlfriend, and so do many of the other characters. I found myself noticing this in a way that I'm certain none of the readers did in 1951, when the book was first published. Would someone today writing a story set in 1951 remember that little detail, especially if they'd been born after smoking restrictions went into effect?

The more I think about it, the more I'm certain it's those little details that would trip a writer up, rather than the larger issues such as racism or cruelty to animals or sexism. Consider adding a look at newspapers or magazines from the time, especially the advertisements. These will clue you in to these small details, enabling you to add a degree of verisimilitude to your work.

The Great Beeswax Experiments

I'm often asked questions like the following: "I'd like to know more about the kinds of research you do – the depth of the research and where you start. I think a lot of people feel that since it's Fantasy or SF, that you 'just make it up.'"

It so happened right around the time I was asked this question, I'd just finished some research that had nothing to do with books or on-line sources. These were The Great Beeswax Experiments.

At the time, I was writing *Artemis Invaded*. There came a point where my characters needed a material that would be flexible, firm, easily molded, and not likely to become brittle or dry out. The level of technology was relatively low, so the synthetic putties and caulks we take for granted aren't available.

Adding to the challenge, my characters were camping out in the wilderness. Visiting a store or shop was not an option. The characters would not have been likely to pack anything like this. This world has some very odd elements, but magic is not one of them, so conjuring what they needed out of thin air wasn't an option.

Clay becomes brittle when it dries out. Since flexibility was needed, baking the clay won't help. Fabric, even packed tightly, wouldn't do the job. Resin (as is naturally extruded by many evergreens) would be too sticky. After some consideration, I decided that beeswax might serve my needs. I'd even established earlier that my characters had gathered some honey. Tah-dah!

Or maybe not, "tah-dah." I started wondering how one worked with something so completely and utterly sticky as honeycomb.

I consulted my friend Rowan Derrick, whose family keeps bees, and asked her how honey was typically separated from the comb. She gave me a nicely detailed briefing, including mentioning that honeybees produce more than one type of wax. Propolis wax is used as a sort of glue for sealing the hive. It is darker in color and harder than the regular wax.

The wax we typically think of as "beeswax" is from the comb proper. The walls of the cells are very light and thin. Rowan explained that there are two ways of separating the wax from the honey. The better method uses draining buckets equipped with a series of sieves. The sieves filter the honey, eliminating "waxy bits," parts of bees, and leaving the honey more free of pollen.

The faster, not-so-good method is to warm the honey slightly so that the honey and wax separate. The wax then floats to the top and hardens as it cools. This, of course, leaves bee parts and other residue in both the wax and the honey (depending on what floats and what doesn't).

Well, as I mentioned above, my characters are camping. I didn't figure they would have brought buckets and sieves with them so,

Wanderings on Writing

despite the drawbacks, if they were separating the honey from the comb, they'd use the warming method. Rowan very kindly offered to give me some wax that had been heated and molded, but that otherwise wasn't overly filtered or processed. The piece she brought me was about two and a half inches by two inches by about an inch thick. It was also very, very hard.

No problem, thought I. *Body heat will warm it.* I put the block of wax into a plastic bag and sat on it. I sat on it for a long while. It got warmer, but it didn't get appreciably softer.

Not so good, thought I. *Maybe body heat isn't enough. Maybe if I set it near something warm, it will soften without melting.* (Melted wax would not be good for my needs.)

I happened to be cooking a very large kettle of soup. I put the block of wax on the metal top of the stove, about a finger's width from the kettle. When I went back later, I dreaded finding a puddle of wax. What I did not expect was to find the wax was as hard as ever.

I spoke about this with Rowan and she commented that the heating process does tend to make the wax harder when it cools. However, wax right from the comb remains soft. The problem is getting rid of the honey. I went to the grocery store and found a brand of honey sold with a piece of honeycomb inside. I happily purchased it.

At home, I fished out the bit of honeycomb and dropped it into a small bowl so any loose honey could run off. I did this several times, getting deliciously sticky in the process. When I felt I had gotten rid of as much honey as possible this way, I considered what to try next. Since the individual cells of the honeycomb are designed to keep out water, dropping the whole thing into a bowl of water to rinse wouldn't work.

Mashing the lot with a fork, then rinsing might work, but it might also cause the wax to harden, especially if the water was very hot. Eventually, I decided on a very primitive technological separation method. From eating honeycomb, I knew that the temperature of a human mouth is not enough to cause the wax to harden. With the edge of a fork, I cut off a piece of honey comb and stuck it in my mouth. Even with much of the honey drained off, it was very sweet.

Gently and patiently, I chewed until I had extracted the honey and was left with a small wad of wax. I repeated this until I had finished the comb, ending up with a chunk of wax about the size of a marble. I let it cool, then tried working it. Cold, the wax was almost as hard as a rock, but body heat was enough to warm it to a workable texture very quickly. At first the wax was a bit grainy and inclined to break, but eventually (probably as I worked the last of the impurities out), it became flexible enough to be shaped.

I then experimented with shaping what I needed. (No. I'm not going to tell you what that was. It could be a major spoiler for a thoughtful reader!) Making what I wanted wasn't quite as simple as I had envisioned but, after some trial and error, I thought I could justify my characters' actions.

Thus endeth the Great Beeswax Experiments.

Could I have just made it up? Said they used beeswax and figured no one would wonder about the details? Possibly, but I think care regarding little details makes for a much more real-seeming book. As I've said before, when you're asking your readers to accept the wildly unlikely (like telepathy or faster than light travel), it's only fair to make sure that other elements are solidly grounded in reality.

And I do think it was one of my more tasty bits of research!

System = Unmagical?

Time and again, when the subject of magic as used in Fantasy fiction arises, I hear the same criticism. This is that systemized magic somehow ruins the "magical" feeling by turning magic into a poor copy of science. "Gamers" are regularly blamed for introducing this element into Fantasy, a criticism that completely disregards the fact that magical systems are as old as the concept of magic itself.

Let's not forget that many of the "classic" Fantasy writers – Jack Vance immediately springs to mind, as does Michael Moorcock – invented magical systems in their stories. Their works pre-dated gaming. Indeed, they influenced gaming. But I wander off topic...

Magical systems are close kin to ritual magic – that is, a magic where a ritual (or system) is used in the belief that following that system will achieve a desired result. Ritual magic permeates numerous cultures. The ancient Egyptians used it not only in those rites associated with death and judgment, but in daily life. (Do you think only mummies wore amulets?). Many European cultures possessed their own forms of ritual magic, dating far back into prehistory. (What do you think cave paintings are?)

Ritual magic is central to many Native American cultures. My husband, Jim, is an anthropologist who specializes in Southwestern cultures. Despite the hard-held belief of many New Age practitioners that the Native Americans are simply "close to nature" and "sensitive to the Great Spirit," magical/religious rituals (there is no real distinction) are integral to the power/belief structures of these peoples. When Jim's division moved into a new building, a member of the staff – who also happens to be a Comanche shaman – gave the building a traditional blessing.

Perhaps no culture so closely equated magic and system as did the Chinese. Moreover, especially to the older Chinese cultures (although plenty of rituals are still practiced today), there was no distinction between science and magic. When the first Chinese emperor was advised to burn all books except for technical manuals and handbooks (the history of his own lineage was excluded from this general attempt to erase all contradictory history and tradition), divination was included with medicine, agriculture, and arboriculture as what we would today term "hard science." (This event is the root of my "Breaking the Wall" series, which begins with *Thirteen Orphans*.)

As a writer of Fantasy fiction, I have explored many types of magic. In my contemporary novels such as *Changer* and *Child of a Rainless Year*, I have dealt with more "numinous" or non-ritual magic. When I designed an imaginary world for my Firekeeper novels, what form of magic was practiced in what region varied according to the culture that colonized an area. Some of these were ritual magics. Some were not.

However, when dealing with historical or living magical traditions – as I did with *Legends Walking* (West African, among others), *The Buried Pyramid* (ancient Egyptian), and *Thirteen Orphans* (Chinese) – I did not ignore the elements of systematized or ritual magic. Rather, I found material within those traditions that was as numinous and mysterious as any vague evocation of magical vibrations could be.

I found the Chinese system particularly fascinating. Over time, an elaborate system of correspondences evolved, so that every significant plant, animal, number, element, star/planet, and suchlike are linked. These links are not simple. For every affiliation, there is an opposition. Yin and yang means that principles, distinct in Western traditions, are blended, so that within darkness there is a tiny bit of light, within the male there is a touch of the female, within the domestic there must be the wild, and so on...

Talk about complex, mysterious, and full of wonder. I loved it!

(Note: An earlier version of this piece appeared on Tor.com in 2008)

Musing on Magical Items

How much is too much when it comes to magical items?

Over the last few years, I've encountered a real resistance among some readers, writers, and editors of Fantasy fiction to novels that include magical swords, amulets, rings, and the like. These works are spoken of with a sneer and are much less likely to get attention when the time comes for award nominations. Oddly, this resistance includes "fan" awards, even when the books in question are topping the bestseller lists.

So, where did this resistance to magical items come from? Why has the idea arisen that the inclusion of such makes a piece less magical?

Certainly magical items belong to Fantasy from its earliest roots in mythology. Many of the Norse gods possessed magical items. Some had more than one. Thor, for example, not only had his hammer, Mjolnir, but also an iron mitten that let him catch the hammer when he threw it at a target. (The hammer apparently had boomerang properties). Thor also had a magical belt that increased his strength two-fold. Oh, yeah, let's not forget his war cart, which was drawn by billy-goats and flew through the air.

Greek myths also contain magical items. These are not limited to those like the Chariot of the Sun, which can be "excused" as a pseudo-scientific explanation for natural phenomena. Nor are they restricted to divinities. Mortal heroes often bear magical weapons. Perseus is equipped with not only Athena's mirror-bright shield, but with Hermes' own magical sword. As if this is not enough, the nymphs of the north loan him magical sandals that let him fly, a cap that makes him invisible, and a bag that swells to contain whatever was put into it, (so he'll have a neat and tidy place to store Medusa's head).

I could go on and on... There are magical harps of the British Isles. The amulets and charms of the Egyptians. The magical armor and weapons with which almost every culture equips its gods and heroes. Sometimes, the ability to use these items is taken as proof that the bearer is, in fact, worthy to be a hero.

So, again I ask, why are such so often scorned when they appear in Fantasy fiction? Why does giving the protagonist a magical sword immediately slide the tale down the literary scale?

I've recently re-read Lloyd Alexander's "Chronicles of Prydain." (The first book is *The Book of Three*, if you're interested in trying them.) Here we have a magical sword, a glowing sphere, and a magical harp... There are magical tomes, potions and lotions, and a very potent amulet. Indeed, the only item in the magical bag of tricks that is missing is a ring.

Despite this, I have heard the books praised by the hardest of the hard-headed as really good Fantasy fiction. Nor do I think that "The Chronicles of Prydain" get away with including magical items because they are "children's books." In fact, as an avid reader of YA fiction, lately I've encountered more – not less – aversion to novels that include magical items. Yes. Even though Harry Potter included a host of such, the resistance is there.

I think there are a couple of reasons this aversion has developed. One is because too many magical items seem to be carbon copies of every other magical item. They are copied in form and abilities but without the emotional resonance. Young Taran is in complete awe of the magical sword wielded by his idol, Gwydion. This awe cannot help but transfer to the reader. However, far too many magical swords seem to come from Swords R Us, without history or mystery.

Penalty is another thing that's often missing. When young Taran impulsively grabs Gwydion's sword, it burns him. Only those of "noble worth" can use this sword. Elric of Melnibone's Stormbringer is even more dangerous. The sense that these swords aren't "one size fits all" items adds to their mystique.

And let's not forget what happens if you play around with the One Ring.

So if you want to use magical items in your stories, make sure you give them a heritage – one that may be fraught with peril. Your story will be all the richer for it.

Mythological Gateway

For me, the gateway to Fantasy and Science Fiction was mythology. Unlike many SF/F readers, I can't tell you what was the first SF/F book I read. Nor am I going to claim to be one of those precocious readers who wasn't even out of diapers before I was reading the encyclopedia.

As far as I know, I learned to read when I was in first grade. Whatever Sister Stephanie did to teach me, she must have done it right. Certainly, my mother must have played a big role in contributing to my enthusiasm. I don't remember her reading to me specifically, but I do remember her reading to me and my siblings. By second grade, Miss O'Donnell was arranging for me to read with her sister's – also Miss O'Donnell, a source of endless fascination for some reason – third graders.

Believe it or not, this is going somewhere...

When I was in third grade, my family moved. The new area's school system had a reputation for being excellent. It might well have been. What it lacked was order and discipline. My parents had no way of knowing how I was doing in third grade because most of the material was a repeat of second grade. My teacher, Mrs. Cox, was a nice woman. She read to us, too. I remember her reading from the Beverly Cleary books about Henry and her laughing so hard that she choked when Henry (in a contest with another boy over who really owns the dog Ribsy) yells something like: "Horsemeat, Ribsy! Horsemeat!"

In fourth grade, my world changed. I was put in what was called an Open Classroom. My teacher was a sweet young thing named Miss Campbell. Her mandate was based on a philosophy that children learn best at their own pace and doing what they want.

They expected me to learn long-division. They gave me a free pass to the library. What do you think I did? I read. That's when I became seriously addicted to mythology. My favorites were the D'Aulaire's lavishly illustrated Greek and Norse myths. I took these out so often I came to think of them as "mine." Later on that same year, I read both the *Iliad* and the *Odyssey* – adult versions – because so many of the characters were already old friends.

Wanderings on Writing

And somehow this led to Science Fiction and Fantasy. As I said, I don't recall my first venture into either. I do remember that one of the reasons I started seeking out SF/F was because of summer reading. Once a week, my mom took us with pretty regular fidelity to the local library. I don't recall her editing our choices. Her only rule was that we could take out as many books as we could carry.

I'd been reading "children's books," but the books I liked (often horse stories or things like Nancy Drew) were bulky and heavy. Science Fiction and Fantasy came in paperbacks, lots and lots of them displayed on a big spinning wire rack. Westerns came in paperback, too. (This rack was up against a wall). I read a bunch of those as well. Oddly, I didn't get into adult Mysteries until a year or so later, when I started babysitting.

However, if weight and bulk considerations led me *to* SF/F, it was SF/F that led me *back* into the hardcover shelves. I still remember the first author whose books I went looking for, going to the card catalog, then to the intimidating, dusty reaches of the adult shelves.

Clifford Simak. I don't remember which book I found there, but when I'd read all the paperbacks the library had of his stories, I had to find more of his odd, twisting perspective.

Oh... And I'm still lousy at long-division, but at least there are calculators to help with that!

Jane Lindskold

Walking Away From It

When I'm stuck on what I'm writing, I walk away and go do something else, preferably something mindless, like chopping up vegetables for dinner or pruning or digging holes.

Walking away from writing is a hard tactic to explain. Most Americans are taught to keep working on a problem: put one foot in front of another and we'll reach our goal. For those writers who have only a limited amount of time in which to write (after the day-job, after the kids are in bed, whatever), walking away practically comes as heresy.

But the fact remains that, for me, staring at a screen or sheet of paper, trying to force the words, is the best way to make sure they'll stay away.

Part of the reason for this is that I'm a subconscious plotter and my subconscious is notoriously cranky about being forced. However, if I get to work on something else, then the subconscious relaxes and often the words start flowing.

This has happened a lot to me, but there's one occasion I think of as the perfect illustration.

I was writing *Changer*. The novel was well past the introductory chapters. Characters were on stage, problems were not only introduced but mounting in complexity. As they did, I began to be troubled by the question of why these people didn't simply bop each other over the head. Instead, some of them had been frustrating each other for millennia.

To place this in context, this was in the day when *Highlander* was very popular both as a movie (which I saw) and a television show (which I never saw). In the universe according to *Highlander*, immortals seemed to have nothing better to do with their time and energy than murder each other. Seemed a waste of immortality to me, but as my characters began to suspect and doubt each other,

Wanderings on Writing

I did wonder why several of the more annoying (Sven Trout, for example) hadn't ended up dead long ago.

I sensed – that's the only way to put it; you'll simply have to believe me – that there was something more than caution staying their hands. However, I couldn't figure it out.

So I shut down the computer and walked out the door to get my daily exercise. I was not even two-tenths of a mile from my front door when the solution came to me. Words came rushing into my head. Images nearly drowned me in their intense complexity. I resisted turning around to get it all on paper. Instead, I went and walked my usual three-mile route.

My feet probably did speed up a bit on the last few blocks. I hurried through the door, grabbed paper, and started scribbling.

Accord and Harmony, the differences between them, the differences between voluntary and involuntary compliance. Why people who viewed each other as enemies would cooperate – or at least find more interesting ways to undo each other than simple murder.

All of it was there, ready to be used but, if I hadn't walked away, I don't think I would have found it that day.

Over the years, I've learned to walk away, but I always walk back. If I didn't, well, then I'd create a whole new problem, wouldn't I?

Jane Lindskold

Messing Up

Have I ever told you that I do work in polymer clay? I do. Oddly enough, it's writing that got me into it. One of the two books that Roger Zelazny left unfinished at the time of his death and I later completed was *Lord Demon*. Kai Wren, the main character, is a potter and glass blower.

When I started the book, I found myself having a little trouble getting into Kai Wren. I decided I needed to know more about his craft to understand him. I read a bunch of books about making pottery and blowing glass. I watched some demos in person, getting the heat of working glass into my blood, the wet fluidity of making pottery into my soul.

In the course of all of this, I learned about polymer clay. Unlike "real" clay, polymer clay can be fired in your home oven. It's affordable, multi-colored (a huge attraction for me), and a fairly forgiving medium. As my last step in getting to understand Kai Wren, I bought a pack of clay and started working with it. The book is long done, but I've never stopped working with polymer clay.

Maybe because I started working with polymer clay in association with my writing, it's also something I continue to associate *with* writing. This is true to a greater or lesser extent with several other crafts I do. All of them occupy my conscious mind so that my subconscious mind is freed up to work on the story in question.

I talked about this a bit in "Walking Away From It." This time, I want to talk about something related but different: The Importance of Messing Up.

The importance of messing up is related to feeling free to take risks, but it's completely different. When you take a risk, you know it might not work. When you mess up, you know you've done something wrong. You've wasted time. You've wasted effort. Where a risk taken that doesn't pay off merits a shrug and an "oh, well," messing up can trigger anger, resentment, a feeling that you'll never get it right.

For any type of project this is dangerous, but for writing it can be devastating. Why? Because writers so often expect to get it right the first time through.

Let me go back to me and polymer clay.

I was working along, blending a color for modeling a figure. I'd gotten it just right. Then I realized I didn't have enough for the project. I pulled out more clay and started blending again. This time, whether it was because I was tired or impatient or just eager to get going, I messed up. I forgot one of the cardinal rules of blending polymer clay. Always add far less of the "darker" or "stronger" color to the lighter. Suddenly, instead of the tawny orange shade I wanted, I had something between flame and pumpkin.

To make matters worse, my hands hurt from all the kneading I'd been doing. I wanted to quit. But, hey, this was just polymer clay. The orange wasn't wasted. I could use it some other day. Instead of quitting, I pulled out more yellow and added a small amount of the pumpkin orange. Eventually, I had my tawny shade. I was out of time to finish that project, but there would be another day.

With writers, however, too often the reaction to messing up is to reject the project entirely. It isn't good enough. It's lost its "magic." Something else would be more fun, easier, more popular.

The thing is, unlike that polymer clay which can be reused, a story rejected because the writer "messed up" is lost forever. The writer really *has* wasted time and effort. I'm not saying every story is worth finishing. Sometimes what is learned from messing up is that this particular piece truly is a dead end. Sometimes, however, in working beyond where you messed up, you can learn a lot, not just about that story but about how you make stories.

So don't be discouraged when you mess up. Come back and give it another try. Maybe you'll need to walk away for a while. Maybe you'll need to categorize the new effort as taking a risk, but at least give it a try. At the very worst, you'll know you didn't just surrender to frustration. At the best, you may have a finished piece where otherwise you'd just have had a sense of disappointment.

Prequels

I'm not certain when the word "prequel" first appeared. "Prequel" isn't in that standard reference *Webster's* 3rd *International Dictionary*, but, then again, my copy has a copyright date of 1971. Nonetheless, as recently as forty years ago, the term "prequel" was not in common use. "Sequel," by contrast, has roots going back to Middle English.

A prequel is different from a flashback in that a flashback is set within what, in the context of the work, is the "present." Flashbacks provide information to help the reader (or viewer) understand present action. This is true even if they make up the majority of the work. A great example of this is Roger Zelazny's novel *Lord of Light*, which is, effectively, a series of flashbacks. These both provide a context for present action and serve to create a considerable amount of suspense since, despite his many attempts, the main character's carefully-crafted rebellions have always ended in failure. Dare the reader hope that the present attempt has any better chance?

By contrast, a prequel is a work that is set in the past of already available works. *Starhawk* by Jack McDevitt is a good example. *Starhawk* is set when Jack's recurring character, Priscilla "Hutch" Hutchins, is a newly-minted interstellar spaceship pilot. It's a good read. McDevitt cannot be accused of overwriting. Indeed, sometimes his prose is so spare I want more. Despite this, he does a great job of creating a living, breathing universe. Most chapters end with something that fills out the larger picture. News headlines are popular, but sometimes the reader gets to eavesdrop on chatroom conversations. Also included are excerpts from Hutch's personal journal.

Starhawk is a successful prequel because it works for people like me who have read all the other "Hutch" books, yet could also be a good introduction to the series for those who haven't yet had the pleasure.

Prequels aren't easy to write because the writer must be careful not to violate what has gone before. *Starhawk* works because, by the time in her life when McDevitt introduced Hutch, she was already a skilled pilot with many flights behind her. It's reasonable that she isn't obsessed with these events, dramatic as they are. They're part of the larger context of her life.

The Stephanie Harrington novels that I've written with David Weber (*Fire Season* and *Treecat Wars*) are a different sort of prequel. They aren't prequels to Stephanie's life – indeed *A Beautiful Friendship* (which Weber wrote solo, although he let me kibitz) starts when Stephanie is only eleven. We couldn't go much further back without writing books like "Stephie Learns to Read" or "Stephie Gets Her First Pet."

Nonetheless, the Stephanie Harrington books are prequels to the events in the mainline Honorverse novels. (Stephanie is Honor's ancestor, a several times great-grandmother.) One of the biggest challenges we faced was keeping both technology and human/

treecat elements in line with what had been presented in Weber's other works. Sometimes this was easy. Other times we had to put in a lot of thought as to why some development or another wouldn't have been discovered in Stephanie's time, but had to wait for Honor's time. Given that there are several hundred years between, we had quite a challenge in front of us. Still, I think the stories worked pretty well.

Another challenge was that Weber had already mentioned certain events in Stephanie's life in the Honor novels. An aficionado of the Honorverse will already have a sense of some of the major events coming up in Stephanie's life. However, when we wrote about her, we had to "forget" what we knew and have Stephanie pursue her various goals with no idea that she would be someone remembered and respected in the far future.

Sometimes a work that wasn't created as a prequel can be presented as such. That's what has happened with Peter Jackson's movies built around the events of J.R.R. Tolkien's novel, *The Hobbit*. *The Hobbit* was actually written before the Lord of the Rings trilogy. However, the movies, with their inclusion of all the extra material taken from other of Tolkien's works, transform the slender novel into a massive prequel to the grand events that will come.

Writers of prequels face stumbling blocks that writers of sequels do not. For one, the reader knows the main character is not at risk of life or limb. Another is the danger of including too many "cute" moments explaining various quirks in the characters' personalities. In *Starhawk*, McDevitt lets us know how Priscilla Hutchins came to be known as "Hutch." While this never really concerned me (after all, who wouldn't prefer "Hutch" as a nickname over, say, "Prissy"), it was sort of fun. However, I felt that the Indiana Jones prequel/flashbacks that explained how Indie got his nickname, his hat, and his fear of snakes turned the character into a joke, rather than what he had seemed – a well-developed person with likes and dislikes.

Wanderings on Writing

On the other hand, a good prequel can fill in things a reader has longed to know about a character or setting that could not be put into the original novel or film without creating a dull info-dump. For example, the Star Wars franchise has successfully produced material about the Clone Wars and other past events that has nicely fleshed out the universe.

A good prequel can even mend problems in the original story. One of my favorite anime series, *SaiYuki*, had a distinctly weak ending. A three-episode prequel entitled *SaiYuki Gaiden* filled in the missing parts. I have to admit, I was very pleased to have some of my guesses confirmed and to finally feel that particular story arc had been given a solid ending – this despite the fact that I knew from later events that the ending could not be a happy one.

Especially if you've put a lot of effort into creating a back-history for your novel, you may figure that a prequel will be easy. However, the reverse is often true. Writing a prequel presents its own set of challenges – but you may find them well worth taking on.

Truth?

Perhaps one of the most interesting questions to ask yourself when designing a major character is what does that person think is "true."

Such issues come up frequently in SF/F. Characters learn that those they've worshipped as gods are mere mortals – perhaps suffering from delusions of grandeur, perhaps kind souls willing to accept the burdens of presumed deity to lead their followers toward higher ideals. Or they learn that what they have taken for "the world" is a spaceship. Or science reveals the existence of parallel universes that lead to questions of what – if anything – is "real" and absolute.

Another popular SF/F gambit is to rewrite some religious, mythological, or historical event in a fashion that provides an alternate explanation for why events unfolded in the manner that they did. Tim Powers does this frequently, interpreting actual historical events so that his interpretation makes more sense than does actual history. A device – such as the Mask featured in Fred Saberhagen's novel, *Mask of the Sun* (and its offspring, the collection *Golden Reflections*, edited by Joan Saberhagen and Bob Vardeman) – might enable probabilities to be manipulated.

Nor do these truths need to be the "big truths" of religious faith or patriotism or some philosophical ideal. Indeed, sometimes the smaller truths define a person even more – and a revelation that violates those small, personal truths can lead to considerable upheaval.

Let's take a character – call him Oscar – who believes with all his heart that his mother was a virtuous woman who was a virgin when she married and never strayed thereafter. What would happen to Oscar if he learned that Mom had had a lover beforehand? Even if that lover had been her future husband, still, if Oscar had lived a life of strict self-discipline because he wanted to live up to his mother's example, then he might feel as if the foundations of his behavior had been shattered. He might wonder if all his self-sacrifice was worth the effort.

Or perhaps Oscar wasn't at all self-disciplined and had spent most of his life lambasting himself for not being able to live up to his mother's example. How would he feel if he learned that the ideal never existed?

What if he found that his virgin angel mother hadn't just "slipped once" but had been far from either virgin or angel? Then how would he react? How would his relationship with his mother change? How would his own behavior change? Would he go wild in reaction? Would he become a sanctimonious prude, determined to show her up?

Don't forget the ripple effect! How would Oscar's relationship with the rest of his family change – especially if he learned that one or more people he trusted had been lying to him? These might have been outright lies or lies of omission – withholding information, rather than directly distorting it. Which would be worse?

Would Oscar be angry? Resentful? Would he feel foolish – wondering if people had been sniggering behind his back all this time? Maybe he'd be a bighearted person who would decide that the failings of long ago are to be forgiven. Still, I wonder if he'd ever trust easily again.

The "truth" doesn't need to be related to sex, of course. Honesty is another area around which "truth" tends to form. What if Oscar had always believed his father had been an honest businessman or politician, then learned that his father had been systematically embezzling or accepting bribes?

What if Oscar was a young knight who strove to live up to the example of his valorous king and ruler only to learn that the king had, in his own days as a fighter, been less than knightly? What if Oscar was a spaceship pilot who believed that the ships he took out into the void were the result of careful construction and meticulous planning, only to learn that the science was dubious, the design haphazard, and his own life viewed as disposable?

What happens when heartfelt truths are neither violated nor betrayed, but come up against other interpretations of reality? Monotheism confronting polytheism, both sincerely believed in, provides good grounds for internal conflict. So does the conflict between sociological or political philosophies such as socialism, capitalism, and totalitarianism.

Leaving aside the "heavy" issues for a moment... Even changes in what is known to be "true" about a thing can be fun. I've always thought that Bilbo wasn't as grimly afraid of the One Ring as he should have been because he couldn't help but think of it as a sort of toy that let him play pranks.

In his charming "Chronicles of Prydain," Lloyd Alexander has the Golden Pelydryn, a powerful magical orb, remain hidden in plain sight, the "bauble" of the young, seemingly frivolous, chatterbox Princess Eilonwy. The odd thing is that, even when everyone in Eilonwy's circle knows that the "bauble" is far more than a bauble, still, truth is not enough to restore to it appropriate wonder and awe.

"What is truth?" asked Pontius Pilate.

Whatever the answer, I'll offer that knowing what truths your characters hold near to their hearts is the best way to make those characters come to life.

Some Thoughts on Designing Aliens

One evening, after looking at my friend Walter Jon Williams' slides from his scuba diving trip to Indonesia, the conversation turned to underwater life forms.

As I probably don't need to tell you, Walter also writes Science Fiction. Given our shared interests, inevitably, alien life forms entered the conversation. After viewing various types of sea turtles and octopi, nudibranchs (lots and lots of these), giant clams, miniature crabs, striped eels, infinite-armed starfish, and bustling cuttlefish – not to mention fish that walked, "flew," and performed elaborate wriggling dances, (as well as a few that merely swam), we all agreed that SF writers who desired to create a truly alien race would do well to depart land and delve into the sea in search of models.

I, for one, would be seriously tempted by the octopus – and not as some sort of horrible monster. They're so very appealing, with their flexible bodies, camouflage coloration, ink clouds, and big eyes. The problem of digits for manipulating their environment is neatly handled – or perhaps I should say "tentacled" – by their eight limbs. I'd enjoy getting into the psychology of a creature who would not have our restrictive ideas of "front and back," for whom an "impassible" barrier would need to be something far more dense than what stops us.

And that's even before evolving my alien from the octopus template, much as humans are evolved from primates. Could there be an effective land octopus? Perhaps an amphibious one. Would they take a page from the hermit crab and design elaborate shells? Mecha-octopi from the deep… Maybe they'd be naturals for space travel.

Compared to some of the creatures Walter showed us, octopi are practically "normal." But there would be a problem with evolving aliens from, say, nudibranchs. For one, how many readers have ever heard of a nudibranch? Before Walter showed them to us, I only knew about them because another friend belonged to a yarn club that used the coloration of different types of nudibranchs as the basis for a challenge to yarn dyers. When a writer starts out needing to lecture the readership, it's a dicey situation. So aliens are often modeled on creatures that can be quickly shorthanded for the reader: reptiles, cats, and canines for the "good guys," spiders and other insects (and often reptiles) for the "bad guys."

Even when a writer tries hard to keep the aliens alien, often they're reduced to the nearest terrestrial equivalent. I am passionately attached to the various alien races in Larry Niven's "Known Space" stories, but I can't help but be saddened by how the Kzinti are often reduced to "tigers in space." I know why... The "real" Kzinti aren't nearly as attractive. The epithet "rat cat" frequently applied to them in the stories is a reminder that their tails are pink and naked. But tigers in space look so much better on the book jacket and, in time, the depiction colors the interpretation of the creature.

Larry Niven often used psychology as much as biology as a model for his aliens. I adore the cowardly Puppeteers. The paranoid Trinocs were fun, too. Then there are weird Outsiders, who sail between the stars without need of ships. Their motivations may be mysterious, but Niven never leaves the reader in doubt that the Outsiders have motivations. Still, it's the rat-cats that everyone comes back to, maybe because they can be more easily understood.

It's been a long time since I read any of C.J. Cherryh's "Chanur" books, but this was another good take on the "cat-like" alien. In this case, she used the idea that in a "real" lion pride the males are idle studs. It's the females who go out and get the dinner. Evolve this forward and you have the Chani and their culture, up to and including shortcomings that mirror (perhaps deliberately) those of the Kzinti.

If I had to pick my favorites among more recent aliens, I'd go straight to Vernor Vinge. His great, fat books need to be fat because there's no "shorthanding" when he creates an alien culture. The Tines, featured in *A Fire Upon the Deep,* are wonderful. Superficially canine, they are actually group minds, a development that permits them to get around the restrictions of not having "hands." Instead they have mouths... lots of mouths, and a lot more range and coordination than the average human.

In Vernor's *A Deepness in the Sky*, he explores (among other things) the human desire to see the "other" as some variation of ourselves. The alien "Spiders" are anything but human, but over and over again the humans who interact with them need to fight the conflicting impulses to see them either as terrifying monsters or as "just like us." Even at the end of the novel, the human who has come closest to understanding Spiders on their own terms finds herself forced to remember how physical orientation alone is enough to create distortions in interpretation: "… human bodies extended upward, and Spider bodies sideways. If she didn't keep a downward 'view' she missed out on 'facial' expressions…"

Great stuff!

So creating an alien – especially if it is to be used as a character, not just window-dressing – is a real challenge. On the one hand, it needs to be alien enough not to just seem like, say, a Japanese samurai in a fur suit – and on the other it needs to resonate enough with the reader that there can be sympathy, interest, and enthusiasm.

Where the Personalities Grow

When I posted "Some Thoughts on Designing Aliens" (under the title "The Alien Sea") on the Wednesday Wanderings, there were many interesting comments, both on the site and off. One of the "ghosts" found herself thinking about a type of alien closer to home: those creatures we call humans. She wondered whether the personality of the writer makes a big difference in how the writer expresses the personalities of different characters. She also wondered how, if it did, the writer could learn to work beyond such limitations.

I think that writers' personalities do influence how writers develop their characters. Initially, in fact, how the characters process situations is likely to be similar to how the writer would do so.

If the writer is introspective, then the character is likely to be so. If the character is impulsive or temperamental, ditto. Nor is this always a bad thing. There's a certain "rightness" about such characters. Moreover, there is a type of reader who seems to want to believe that, even when reading fiction, they are actually reading thinly-shrouded autobiography. Nothing seems to excite this sort of reader more than finding out that a writer "really" plays the bagpipes or is an expert on wines or practices a particular marital art, just like the protagonist does.

If I'm writing a story with an ensemble cast, my characters tend to discuss events. I don't doubt that this is because that's what I would do in a similar situation. However, I also write this way because I think it's a lot more interesting for the reader to be part of a discussion than to be told by an abstract narrative voice: "After much discussion, the characters decided to raid the lair of the Bat King." Especially if there had been some disagreement as to the wisdom of confronting this awesome monster, as a reader, I'd like to know why they made that choice.

To this day, for example, the council scene in *The Fellowship of the Ring* is one of my favorite parts of the novel. Not only do we find out why a certain course of action was chosen, we learn a lot about how various characters reacted to the decision to attempt to destroy the One Ring. Do I like this scene because Tolkien wrote it well or because it resonates with my sense of what's right? Good question.

Wanderings on Writing

For a writer to grow, the writer must eventually move outside of his or her own narrow frame of reference. As much as we'd like to believe so, everyone is *not* like us. Different people react to different situations, well, differently.

This was brought home to me afresh some years ago when I ended up being the nexus of a rather nasty situation. I was extremely frustrated because none of those involved were sitting down and talking as a group. Instead, people were phoning each other or, occasionally, e-mailing each other. As a nexus, I heard a lot of different points of view and, eventually – because it was physically impossible to get everyone into one place – I composed an e-mail outlining the situation as I saw it, placing the blame for starting the problem firmly where it belonged.

I thought clarifying the situation would enable matters to be reset and we could all get back to work. Thank heavens I ran my proposed e-mail by a close friend who was also involved in the situation. Her response was to say calmly, "And what do you think this will do? Do you expect them to say, 'Right, we've behaved badly. Sorry.'?"

I admitted that this was precisely what I expected... After all, I'd outlined the facts and the facts pretty neatly showed how the situation had developed. In the background I came from, this would have at the very least led to an admission of how the misunderstanding had developed and a chance to start the discussion afresh and maybe repair the damage. My friend said, "Jane, that's because you come from a family of lawyers. Not everyone accepts such discussion in that way. You're more likely to make everyone defensive and things will get worse."

What an eye opener! What a view into a different mindset! What a *great* thing for a writer!

The e-mail was never sent but, to this day, when writing characters I remind myself to delve into personalities and insecurities, to play with how, in certain social situations, such illogical things as having been an insecure wallflower in tenth grade might make a currently competent business executive behave like a junior high school student.

So, short of cultivating conflict and studying reactions, how can a writer expand his or her psyche to embrace personalities other than his or her own?

One way is to make a study of the people close to you and try to understand not only how but why they react as they do to certain situations. Agatha Christie's autobiography is far from being (as are the autobiographies of so many writers) a thinly-disguised, "How I Became the Famous Writer I Am Today." In fact, page for page, she talks very little about her writing, and, when she does, it's almost always in the context of some other aspect of her life.

However, for a reader who has read a considerable amount of Agatha Christie's work, her autobiography holds revelations as to how and why she kept returning to certain types of people in her writing. The attractive ne'er-do-well owes a great deal to her brother. Her abiding interest in older people was clearly influenced by the two elderly aunts who lived with her family. Her ex-husband, Archie, may be the reason she writes betrayers so well. Her father provides the affectionate template for characters who cannot adjust to the times. And, of course, her deep understanding of the archeologist comes from her second husband, Max Mallowan.

However, Dame Agatha did not merely recycle her life into story-shaped jigsaw puzzles. She made the effort to understand these people (and many others), to learn what motivated them, and then to use that to create rich suites of characters whose interactions – no matter how superficially illogical – become logical when you get into their heads.

Some writers make the jump from their own point of view more easily than do others. Those who are fascinated by the other, the alien, the stranger – whatever term you choose to give it – are more likely to start this exploration earlier but, for a writer to grow, I believe that he or she must eventually develop, as did Kipling's Kim, two (or more) sides to their head.

One Person, Many Faces

Developing character personalities is more complex than the simple question I addressed in "Where the Personalities Grow." Just to remind you, that question was "Do writers write characters with personalities like their own and, if so, can they develop beyond that point?"

My answer was yes and yes, and I talked a little bit about why I thought so. However, as I was moving to the end of that piece, I realized that there was a lot more to writing realistic characters than this. One thing that struck me was that it's a rare person who is the same in all situations, with all sorts of people. However, all too often, characters in stories are one sort of person and react to all situations and people in the same way.

Now, this isn't always a bad thing. I'm quite fond of Robert Parker's novels about Spenser. What kept me reading them through the last novel Parker wrote before his death was my fondness for the characters – especially the core three: Spenser, Hawk, and Susan. Of these three, Spenser and Hawk could be said to be the sort of people who react in the same manner to all situations. They're tough, reliable, socially savvy, and smart. Spenser is both less tough and less smart than Hawk – Hawk never would have gotten shot in the way Spenser does in *Small Vices* – but that's okay. Spenser has other qualities that may make him stronger than Hawk overall. But, whether faced with a big problem or a small one, they react in a consistent fashion.

There is a comfort to reading about characters like this. Mystery and Thriller protagonists in particular are often of this type. No matter their quirks or shortcomings, they'll come through in the end, upholding whatever their variation on justice might be.

Maybe there are "real" people like this, too, but if so, I haven't met many. Most real people change according to who they are with and the circumstances in which they find themselves.

One good example is what I'll call the "wolf pack alpha" type. This is the sort of person who is usually at the core of a social group. Like a good wolf pack alpha, they're only dominant in the best sort of way – that is, they arrange situations for the greater benefit of the social group. Someone only observing them in that context might think them strong, confident, and self-assured.

However, change the situation, add in someone who this sort of "alpha" views as dominant over him or her – a boss, a potential benefactor, someone they see as more important than themselves – and they become not a leader but a follower. Suddenly, instead of setting up the situation for the good of the group as a whole, they are more interested in winning the favor of this new alpha. In a worst-case scenario, the former alpha may begin to bully subordinates who once could trust in their leader's protection.

That's why I call this type a "wolf pack alpha" because, as in a wolf pack, behavior changes according to who is perceived to hold the power. But wolf pack alphas are not bullies (except in certain situations). They really do care about the strength of their group, because they perceive themselves within a group context.

Bullies are the perfect type of the character whose behavior shifts according to the situation and their perception of power. Spenser and Hawk are not above beating someone up if that's the best way to handle a situation – but this attitude does not change depending on who is watching or what the penalty might be. A bully, by contrast, changes like the wind.

One of the best bullies I've ever encountered in fiction is Hakeswill from the Sharpe stories by Bernard Cornwell. When the commanders are around, Hakeswill is militarily correct, even a touch groveling. However, when the bosses are absent, he is cruel to the point of sadism. The actor who brought this character to the screen handled his role so well that – I'll admit it – I was continuously on edge in those stories in which he appeared.

Bullies are common in middle grade and YA fiction. Lots of the tension in the Harry Potter stories derives from various bullies – both adult and younger. However, bullies are less often used in adult fiction, except for the obvious, swaggering thugs. As I see it, a good bully is often a smart character, if rarely likeable. An adult bully – even a thug – needs to be careful of the consequences of being caught.

Sometimes, situation is what changes a character's personality. Jack Aubrey in Patrick O'Brien's wonderful sea sagas is exactly the man you want in command of your ship. However, put him on land – especially if matters of pretty women or money are in the offing – and trouble will arise.

Another way in which character personalities can change from situation to situation are patterns based on longtime relationships and, to some extent, differences in age. I've seen many a confident, even blustering, adult, change entirely when a parent is present. The change might be something as minor as a person who normally swears or dresses provocatively moderating that behavior in a parent's presence. It might be as drastic as a resumption of subordinate behavior on the part of someone who is normally dominant.

The television show *WKRP in Cincinnati* used this to good comic effect in the relationship between Mr. Carlson and his mother. The impending arrival of "Mother" is enough to turn Carlson into a quivering jelly. However, as the series progressed, Carlson – in part because of the confidence instilled in him by becoming part of the WKRP team – learns to stand up to his mother, a change that makes both him and her happier people.

If you're looking for models of characters who change according to who they are with, you can do far worse than indulge in the various stories of P.G. Wodehouse. Bertie Wooster and his "man" Jeeves are Wodehouse's best-known characters, but the pattern extends throughout Wodehouse's canon.

Confident and even dashing in the company of his peers, Bertie is rendered spineless by his Aunt Agatha. His Aunt Dahlia gets him repeatedly into trouble. However, neither Aunt Agatha nor Aunt Dahlia have any actual power over Bertie. He is independently wealthy, has his own place of residence, and a large social circle.

Aunt Agatha dominates him because she always has done so and Bertie has not changed beyond those childhood patterns. Except for Aunt Dahlia's occasional threats to withhold the pleasure of her dinner table, she is more likely to convince Bertie to participate in one her of wild schemes by appealing to his strong affection for her. Bertie's friends also have no real hold over him, but the plaintive cry "We were at school together" is enough to get him in over his ears. So in a single short story, Bertie may be the suave man of the world, the quivering child, the exasperated peer, and the goggle-eyed romantic. One man, many faces...

Not every character needs to be developed in such detail, but certainly protagonists need a bit more fleshing out. Even a relative monolith like Spenser has endearing little details that make him seem more real. After all, who would expect a former boxer and cop turned private eye to be a gourmet chef?

Wanderings on Writing

Light, Not Necessarily Fluffy

A while ago, I read several books about Winston Churchill. Oddly enough, that started me thinking about fiction, light and dark, and the role both play in our lives.

I'd been interested in Churchill in an abstract fashion since I was a kid. Every second house seemed to have a set of his WWII chronicles, bound in red and white and black, their stirring titles (*Triumph and Tragedy*, *The Gathering Storm*) sounding more like novels than history. Despite this, I didn't know much about Churchill other than the pictures of the weary-looking big man with the cigar. I'd also heard a few stirring quotations and a few caustic jokes credited to him. The one biography I had read felt like one of those tiny samples they give you in the deli when you want taste their potato salad.

When I decided to amend this, the two books our library had as MP3 audio downloads were not about the Winston Churchill of those pictures and quotes at all. Martin *Gilbert's Churchill: A Life, Part One* focused on Churchill's early life, from his boyhood through 1918. The next one, William Manchester's *The Last Lion Alone: Winston Spenser Churchill, 1932-1940*, focused on Churchill's "years of exile."

Although Churchill had risen to First Lord of the Admiralty during WWI and remained in Parliament thereafter, for many years he was far from a mover and shaker. Most of his contemporaries thought he was washed up. His income came from the phenomenal amount of non-fiction he wrote – and even that wasn't enough to sustain his lifestyle. When the Nazi threat became something that couldn't be ignored and changed Churchill's fortunes, he actually had his country house on the market.

For someone like me who knew Winston Churchill as a great and influential politician, perhaps one of the last who merited the title "statesman," it was a shock to learn that he was a sixty-five-year-old "has been" when he was at last, reluctantly, given a Cabinet seat.

But you can read about Churchill elsewhere...

Even as I was listening to these books (the Manchester one alone ran thirty-five hours), I found myself thinking how differently I would have reacted if I hadn't known that Churchill would be vindicated, that his faith that he would someday be able to serve his country in her hour of need (a hope expressed in numerous letters) would come to pass. Even knowing – maybe especially knowing – the larger historical context, I found myself frustrated. I knew the story would have a "happy ending," but getting there was a real trial.

That got me thinking about the expectations we bring to fiction – and about different purposes that different types of fiction serve in helping us to deal with our lives. Even light fiction or adventure fiction serves a very good, very solid purpose – other than the "escape" that most readers of such sheepishly admit they are longing for when they curl up with a much re-read favorite or a book they know isn't going to end with death, doom, and destruction. "Light" in this context doesn't mean without thoughtfulness or merit, any more than a Shakespearean comedy is a laugh a minute.

Recently, a friend mentioned that because his job has been very stressful and demanding, he'd been reading a considerable amount of Georgette Heyer. Heyer specialized in historical romance novels, usually (although not always) set during the English Regency. In them, love will conquer all sorts of obstacles:

class differences (or perceived differences), income gaps, misunderstandings of heroic proportions, and more. No matter how complicated the plot, by the end, the right guy and right girl will have found their way to love – and the promise of a future that will allow them both to flourish.

Trite? No. I wouldn't say that. We all have learned that there are times that love won't conquer all. Is there anything wrong with remembering that you really love someone and so maybe you need to work a bit harder? Is there anything wrong with love being an inspiration to better things? I don't think so.

I'm not much of a fan of romance novels, although I like stories where romance is an element. However, I'm drawn to stories where love in its many forms becomes a driving force. I like "buddy" stories. I like action or war stories, where not letting down the side drives the characters beyond what they thought they could achieve. I found Dumas' *Count of Monte Cristo* incredibly compelling because it's a story about hatred and revenge in which the main character – who has every reason to hate with every fiber of his being – also learns to conquer that hatred.

Light reading? Escapism? Call it that if you will. I think I'd call it healing, a reminder that although life has ground you down, the good things do exist, even if at that moment they seem out of your reach. After Roger Zelazny (with whom I was living at the time) died, I was seriously depressed. I read an enormous amount of Terry Pratchett. (Seriously, I think I read everything Pratchett had published to that point, courtesy, largely, of Jan and Steve Stirling, who handed over boxes containing their entire collection; I've now bought my own copies.)

It wasn't Pratchett's humor that lifted my heart. It was that his stories reminded me of why we love, even though love can hurt you worse than anything. When my dad, my grandfather, and several beloved pets all died within a few months, again, it was to "light" fiction I turned for the building blocks of healing.

Jane Lindskold

What about dark fiction? Oh… I read that, too. But that's its own topic.

Darkness Has Its Place

In "Light, Not Necessarily Fluffy," I talked about how light, escapist fiction may not be so escapist at all. Does this mean I don't like fiction that deals with darker issues? Not in the least. I will admit that the outcome of the story will have a lot to do with whether I decide to go back to the story at some future date, but even with those books I know I'll never read again or movies I won't watch again, I often take away something that makes me think.

If light stories remind us *why* we live, dark stories often supply the tools that help us forge ahead when living seems to be too demanding. Frodo's anguished determination as he slogs through Mordor. Or Tell Sackett's lone stand against those who murdered his wife and now want him out of the way. Or… We all have stories that inspire us, even – maybe especially – in their darkest parts.

One of the greatest compliments I ever received was in a series of e-mails from a reader who told me that my Firekeeper books had kept her going during a really bad time in her life. I assumed this was because the books had let her escape. The final e-mail I received from her showed differently. She mentioned that she was going on a trip to Europe with her mother and that, although she was afraid of going to strange places and of snakes and of several other things, she was "going to be like Firekeeper and be brave."

Wanderings on Writing

Even those dark stories in which the challenges aren't mighty and heroic can be wonderfully heartening. When I was in high school, I read Alexander Solzhenitsyn's novel, *One Day in the Life of Ivan Denisovich*. This story has remained with me all my life, serving as a talisman about trying to find victory even when surrounded by what looks like defeat.

For those of you who aren't familiar with the tale, it recounts one day spent by Alexander Denisovich Shukhov, a prisoner in the Stalin-era Siberian labor camps. The final paragraphs, in which Shukhov seeks value where most would concentrate on the horrible conditions in which he lives (including the fact that he's imprisoned for no justifiable reason at all), are worth quoting. Here they are in Ralph Parker's translation:

> *"Shukhov went to sleep fully content. He'd had many strokes of luck that day: they hadn't put him in the cells; they hadn't sent his squad to the settlement; he'd swiped a bowl of kasha at dinner; the squad leader had fixed the rates well; he'd built a wall and enjoyed doing it; he'd smuggled that bit of hacksaw blade through; he'd earned a favor from Tsezar that evening; he'd bought that tobacco. And he hadn't fallen ill. He'd got over it.*
>
> *"A day without a dark cloud. An almost happy day.*
>
> *"There were three thousand, six hundred, and fifty-three days like that in his stretch. From the first clang of the rail to the last clang of the rail.*
>
> *"Three thousand, six hundred, fifty-three days.*
>
> *"The extra three days were for leap years."*

Nor did I stop with this fictional account with this very qualified "happy" ending. I also read Solzhenitsyn's very long *Gulag Archipelago*. Powerful stuff. Horrible stuff. Frightening stuff. Inspiring stuff.

Jane Lindskold

There are other dark stories that have nothing to do with overt violence, rape, and mayhem. A tale like *Citizen Kane* is about forgetting what you really care about – in that, it's very depressing. It's also uplifting, if you choose to take from it a reminder of what you do care about.

Going back to Winston Churchill for a moment. (See "Light, Not Necessarily Fluffy" for what Churchill has to do with this.) His life wasn't a novel. Readers bring expectations to novels – and believe me, I'm still getting angry fan mail from readers who feel I violated their expectations as to whom Firekeeper should have settled down with!

The boy Winston didn't know as he struggled with his erratic academic career (at one point, his father despaired of him as sub-intelligent) that he would be remembered as a brilliant writer and historian. The young Winston, who broke with the Conservatives on matters of principle, didn't know that twenty years later, he'd be welcomed back. The political "exile" didn't know that exile would end. As far as Winston knew, he – like his father – would find that standing up for his principles would mean his political career was over.

One of the things that sustained Winston Churchill through all of this were stories: stories about idealism and heroism, stories about friendship, stories about valor. He was a historian, and so knew all too well how vicious humans could be to other humans. However, he chose his models and tried to live up to them – even when he was aware of how often he failed.

Now, I'll admit, I don't particularly like reading stories about nasty people doing even nastier things to other people, but I can find value in them. When I find myself getting upset, I look at why I'm so offended by the content. Often, in the process, I learn what I value. That's worth something in itself.

When I was in college, Stephen R. Donaldson's "Chronicles of Thomas Covenant" were on everyone's "must read" list. As the series unfolded, I noticed something interesting. Darkness, grittiness, and edgy content weren't enough to sustain the readership. As Covenant refused to learn and grow, the series lost readers… It never recovered.

In fact, I suspect that most readers of "dark" fiction are waiting for the light at the end of the tunnel. Without it, there's nothing to see.

When It's There... But It Isn't!

Sometimes the author is the worst person for seeing his or her own work clearly. I had this brought home to me when a break in my schedule gave me time to go re-read the opening of one of my "hobby books." (This is a book that I write not to fulfill a contract, but because the idea grabs hold and won't let me go.)

This was a book that I'd talked about frequently. I always describe it in the same way. You can imagine my shock when I went back to re-read the manuscript and discovered that, other than the first sentence, it didn't start at all like I remembered.

I was stunned. This was my story. It has been read by several people, all of whom have loved it. How could I have been so out of touch with what was actually on the page?

As I said above, sometimes writers are the worst people for seeing their own work clearly. Why? Because the writer not only sees what is on the page, the writer also knows what the writer meant to put on the page. Sometimes it all makes it there. Sometimes it doesn't. Sometimes it's there but in the wrong order, and needs to be brought in either earlier or later.

In cases like this, a good editor is very valuable. My first editor was John Douglas, then at Avon Books. The first novel we worked on was *Brother to Dragons, Companion to Owls*. John had bought the novel, so obviously he liked it. However, when the time came for his input he said: "I think this book needs one more chapter."

I was astonished. I'd finished the story. Why did it need more? When I went back and looked the novel over, I realized John was right. He trusted me to find out what should be in the final chapter. Interestingly, over the years, I've had many readers comment to me about details from that last chapter. Clearly, that last bit brought something important to the story.

So, as Betwixt and Between might have said, "Two heads are better than one!"

For my novel *When the Gods Are Silent,* John again offered a valuable insight: "The characters need fleshing out. I think you believe you said more about them than you've put on the page. Just go through and look. See if you think I'm right."

I was sure John was wrong and dove into the manuscript with the passion of a zealot to prove my point. What I realized was that John was right. Details were missing or weren't as well-emphasized as they should have been. I went back and added elements that made the characters what I had imagined them to be.

I'll take my comment one step further and say that a good editor *who has not been working on the project from conception forward* is very valuable to a book. I think this is where writers' groups often fall short. Often, everyone in the group has talked about the book or story in question so often they stop seeing what's on the page and see instead what they know should be there. I don't have anything against writers' groups, but I do think there is a time when a virgin reader is needed.

Overexposure is one reason I dislike presenting proposals. How can the editor judge the actual work if he or she knows what's supposed to be there before reading the actual work? Interestingly, the times I have caught otherwise good editors as flat-out wrong have been in circumstances where they knew something about the piece in advance of reading it.

In these cases, when the editor said something was missing, I was able to show exactly where the "missing" element was, where it was emphasized, and all the rest. The problem was, having seen proposals, having discussed material with me, and – at least I have wondered – having formed a subconscious impression of how the material would be presented, the editor didn't see what was actually on the page.

Still, it's the author's responsibility, not the editor's responsibility to make sure the content of the page reflects the vision. Don't waste time or emotional energy justifying yourself. Revise!

How Do You Do It?

I often get asked questions about my writing process. These questions are often like the following:

> "I know you don't outline. But do you edit at all as you write? Do you do an entire draft and go back through it? How many times do you go through the book before it

goes to an agent or editor? How far along is it before Jim reads it? How much does his feedback factor in? What other first readers do you count on?

Answer 1: I don't outline. Really. Before I start a novel, I have a general feeling about it, but I really don't know where it's going until shortly before I get there. However, I do organize, pretty stringently. I call this process "Reverse Outlining." There's another essay in here dealing with what I mean by that, so I won't go over it again.

Do I edit as I write? Yes. However, this tends to be minimal (altering a word or two). I've known writers who begin their writing day by re-reading what they wrote the day before and carefully grooming it. Then they move onto the next day's writing. I do that occasionally, but usually only when I need to jog my memory as to where I was last session. Otherwise, I pick up where I stopped and go on from there.

Answer 2: Yes. I pretty much write an entire draft of a novel (or short story) before I go back through it. There are two exceptions. One is if I have a major interruption in the writing process, such as a long trip or a several weeks' break because another writing obligation comes up. Then I need to go back and find out what I've actually written, in contrast to what I'd thought about writing. If my reverse outline is up to date, sometimes I just consult that.

Answer 3: How many times do I go through a manuscript before I send it off to my agent or editor? At least twice, often three times. The first review is on the computer. In this reading, my primary goal is to fill in details I left out. I've never been a writer who slows down the flow of a good yarn because I can't remember the color of a secondary character's hair or the day of the week or suchlike. When I come to such a point, I slam in square brackets, sometimes with a note to myself inside them like [color?] and keep going with the story.

Wanderings on Writing

This on-computer reading is also where I check continuity and tighten prose, removing duplicate descriptions and other elements that creep in when (for the writer) weeks have passed, whereas for the reader only a chapter or so has gone by.

I do my second read-through on a hard copy of the manuscript. This is a step I never, ever, ever skip. I seat myself squarely at the table with no fewer than two red pencils at hand and a red pen in case I want to write an additional paragraph. (I write faster in ink than in pencil.) I am as ruthless as possible in this reading: cutting, augmenting, rephrasing, whatever it takes.

Back when I was first getting started, I'd often read the manuscript aloud. There's no better way to catch clunky sentences or omissions. I still do this with short stories. An added bonus is that reading a manuscript out loud is great training for giving public readings.

Another reading of sorts occurs when I am incorporating my changes into the manuscript. This forces me to take another close look.

Answer 4: How far along is the manuscript when Jim reads it? How much does his feedback factor in? Jim doesn't see the manuscript until I'm done with these first two or three readings and have made all the corrections. Basically, he doesn't see the story until it's as good as I can possibly make it.

Occasionally, if I like a particular line or something, I might read it to him. He's very patient about hearing parts of novels with no context. However, I don't look for feedback as I write.

Jim's feedback is very important. Although it might surprise those who think of archeologists as mere grubbers in the dirt, a lot of the work involves writing. Since Jim's a project director, he also does a considerable amount of editing. So I'm really lucky in that my first reader is both a writer and a professional editor.

If I disagree with one of Jim's comments, I make a note of it. If I hear the same comment from another reader, then I take it as a given that I have failed in some way to communicate my intent. Then I will do my best to clarify the point.

Answer 5: What other first readers do I count on? This varies from book to book, based on who has time and who I can trust to be ruthless with me, if such is called for. Much as I love hearing that I'm someone's favorite author or that I write wonderful books, such praise isn't helpful when a book is still in the evolving stages. Heck, even questions about a book that's published can be useful. Sometimes, if I've left something out, I can put it in later in the series (assuming there is a series). Reader comments aren't always useful because some readers want to dictate a direction for the series that I never intended, but I'd rather have them than not.

Another important thing I look for in a first reader is a familiarity with Science Fiction and Fantasy as a genre. Readers who don't know the conventions of the genre may praise where praise isn't really due. (I remember a long-ago colleague who was fascinated by my use of the term "credits," rather than money in *Smoke and Mirrors*.) Or they may get flummoxed by some standard genre element and want more explanation than is due.

Answer Six: Wait! There was no Question Six. But let me add a little more.

I can't polish until I'm done because, until I'm done, I don't know where I'm going. I also get to know my characters better on that first part of the journey. That means I can brush-stroke them into fuller life in later pass-throughs. If I get interrupted somewhere in the composition process, I've been known to go and read through what I wrote before I start again. Inevitably, this will lead to some preliminary polishing but, even if I've done that, I start with the first line and re-read all the way through as part of my self-edit.

Wanderings on Writing

By contrast, I know of writers who anguish over every word, every character name, every descriptive detail. They can't move forward until these parts are perfect. This means their first draft is much, much "cleaner" than mine ever are. Interestingly, many of the writers I know who write this way also belong to writer's groups, so they receive input along the way.

On a tangent... Always beware of writers who talk about not rewriting. This term can mean very different things to different types of writers.

Roger Zelazny often spoke of himself as "not rewriting." Then he made me a gift of a novella typescript. (To the end of his life, he composed either longhand or on a typewriter, never on a computer.) To my surprise, the typescript was full of little cross-outs and changes. I said, "I've heard you say you don't rewrite!" Roger was astonished. "But this is just polishing. When I say 'rewriting,' I mean the type of redrafting I've heard other writers talk about, where they change entire scenes or eliminate entire plots."

In fact, revising and reworking is just as much a part of writing as putting down the original words or brainstorming the plot. Whether you do it as you go along or wait until the end is up to you – but do it!

Getting Feedback, Taking Criticism

My inoculation to the fact that feedback would not always be positive came pretty early on. I have mentioned that I've been really lucky in having a family who reads my stuff. That doesn't mean they always like it...

Jane Lindskold

I remember with twisted fondness my mother's reaction to my first published short story, "Cheesecake," which came out in *Starshore* magazine. I gave copies to both my parents. I don't recall if my father ever said anything, but my mother's contribution remains vivid.

I'd come to her house for some gathering or other. The first guests to arrive were old family friends. Mom pulled the magazine from a shelf and thrust it at the guests, both hands extended: "Look! Jane has published a story! I don't like it very much, but she's published a story!" Her evident pride took away any sting and made me giggle. Later, I learned she'd shared that magazine with just about everyone she thought might be even vaguely interested.

But for all her maternal pride, she was honest in her reaction.

So, the first question you'd better ask yourself before you solicit a reader's reaction is: Am I looking for a critical response or do I just want to be praised?

If you're looking for praise, take it and keep your peace. Don't beg for more. Don't ask, "But didn't you really, really like Bob?" Or "Wasn't the plot twist at the end of chapter four brilliant?"

If you want a critical response, what form do you want it to take? We're going to assume that you're writing with the intention of sharing your work beyond the audience of yourself. Therefore, the goal of feedback is to learn if you've gotten your personal vision across to someone else.

I had a long chat about this with my friend and fellow writer, Sally Gwylan (*A Wind Out of Canaan*). I solicited her opinion specifically because our approaches to writing and feedback differ greatly. Sally has belonged to several writer's groups and finds getting feedback along the way very helpful. By contrast, I don't want any feedback until the work is done and I've made the piece as strong as I possibly can.

119

Wanderings on Writing

Despite Sally and my different approaches, our thoughts overlapped a great deal. We both agreed that it's important to remember that anyone who is reading your manuscript is doing you a terrific favor. They're taking time to read your stuff that they could have spent on something else. If you've solicited comments, they're making notes and circling things. They'll probably go over the piece more than once. Therefore, it's important that you provide some guidelines for what you hope to get out of the process.

Many writer's groups have the rule that the author of a specific piece can't argue with each and every comment. The author should listen, take notes, and then answer politely – or not at all, at least not until enough time has gone by that the emotional reaction can balance with the intellectual.

It's absolutely fine if the writer doesn't like or agree with the comments. However, remember, the people providing the feedback – especially if they are not being paid for their service – are doing you a favor. Take time to think. If you disagree, try to explain why politely.

My husband, Jim, is always my first reader. I've promised him that, even if I disagree with one of his comments, I will write it down. If I hear the same thing from another person, then I will face the fact that although I thought I'd made my point, obviously I didn't do so as clearly as I thought I had and changes need to be made.

This becomes a bit more problematical when the comments are coming from a group, because it is human nature for members of a group to react to each other. For this reason, it's a good idea for group members to prepare notes in advance and that these be given to the writer. That way, the writer has to face that the reaction isn't just crowd psychology.

I've been told I like to argue about comments.... I'm not sure I see my response as "arguing." I want to explain, absolutely.

Jane Lindskold

Especially if someone tells me I didn't put something on the page that I'm sure is there, I want the chance to show them. I don't see that as arguing, but as creative give and take. Not everyone agrees.

Because people react differently to giving and taking criticism, you should choose your critiquers carefully. Not all are created equal. Also, a critiquer who is good for one type of writer may not be good for another. For example, there are critiquers who cannot comment without telling you how they would write the piece. If you're a bit at a loss, this can be great and stimulate new approaches. If you have, however, told the story you want-ed to tell, this will be less than welcome – in fact, you may feel inclined to say, "If that's the story you want, go write it. Leave mine alone."

This is probably a good time to emphasize that if you're looking for criticism, you should make certain that your reader shares an interest in the type of fiction you're writing. This is truer in Sci-ence Fiction and Fantasy than in most genres, since SF/F has its own complex vocabulary and understood literary conventions.

Sometimes, working with the same people can create a shared ethos. If this is indeed shared, then all is well and good. Some-times, however, a writer can be overwhelmed by other people's strong opinions as to what a story should say, how it should be structured, and a million other details. In fact, the stories from a group often begin to have a curious sameness – a criticism that I have heard leveled at the end results of certain writers' work-shops as well.

A good friend of mine tells how when he was writing his first novel, he fell in with a group of people who believed that a book wasn't strong and mature unless at least one major character died. Reluctantly, he violated his own vision and killed off a main character. This, of course, distorted his vision for the story and, in the end, it was not the story he wanted to tell. He has said that someday he'll re-write it and follow his own Muse.

Wanderings on Writing

But does this mean you should not take negative feedback or suggestions for how you might change? Not at all! I've been very grateful to editors – professional and not – for their suggestions, but the suggestions I accepted were those that made my vision more clear. I have never changed the thrust of a story to fit someone else's ethos – and I would hate it if anyone changed his or hers to fit mine.

This means that, to benefit from criticism, you need to have a vision for your story. Without that, even the best criticism in the world won't do you any good. If you don't know what you're trying to do, there's no way a reader can tell you. Don't ask until you're prepared to listen.

Titles Meant?

This past week I finished the three volume *Lumaterre Chronicles* by Melina Marchetta. It's a pretty good series. I have quibbles, but I certainly am glad I took the time to read the books. The thing is, I never would have even picked the books up if my friend Julie hadn't mentioned really liking them.

The titles certainly never would have caught my attention. The first is *Finnikin of the Rock*. What's a "Finnikin"? It turns out to be a person's name, but (based on the cover photo) it could as easily be a sword. (A young man's face and a sword are all that is pictured on the cover.) And what's the 'rock'? A band? A group or nation? A place? (It turns out to be a place.) Not exactly captivating.

Jane Lindskold

The second book in the series is *Froi of the Exiles*, and the third *Quintana of Charyn*. As titles, these have a little more going for them, but only if you've read the first book and know who Froi and Quintana are. "Exiles" has a certain emotive ring to it but, coupled with the nonsense word "Froi," it's not exactly a hook. (And the covers repeat the same motif – a face and a bladed weapon – so they're not exactly a help.)

I had the same complaint about the title for another of Marchetta's novels, *Jellicoe Road*. I adored *Jellicoe Road*. As was my custom when trying a new author, I first took the book out from the library. As soon as I finished it, I went out and bought a copy. However, the title certainly would never have caught my attention.

Titles, it seems to me, are pretty important. A good title might draw a new reader in. A poor title might push a reader away.

My favorite example of this comes from Tim Powers' novel, *Drawing of the Dark*. I'd already read and enjoyed some of Powers' novels, but when I saw a friend reading this one, I flinched away. The title reminded me of dozens of carbon copy Tolkienesque Fantasy novels in which some Dark Lord is doing Bad Things because, if he wasn't, there wouldn't be a novel. Happily for me, the friend told me I was an idiot and loaned me the novel. I loved it. (The "dark" of the title turns out to be beer.) I now own a copy.

Lots of elements can go into creating an effective title. One possibility is to use a word or words that are freighted with emotion or symbolism. "Twilight" is one of these. As a title, this tells a reader nothing, but as a word it packs a wallop.

Game of Thrones is a really good title. "Game" is active. "Thrones" tells you what the prize is and something about the setting. In combination, there is even a hint of irony, since the passage of a throne should never be a game. All good.

Wanderings on Writing

Moonheart is a great title. Both "moon" and "heart" are words that hold a lot of emotion and symbolic impact. Charles de Lint could have chosen to call the book "Lorcalon," which is the actual name given to the "heart of the moon" song his protagonist uses to call upon her inner power, but he had the sense to see that "lorcalon" would mean nothing and might turn readers away, rather than drawing them in.

How the first "Harry Potter" book ended up with two titles is an interesting tale. The original British title was *Harry Potter and the Philosopher's Stone*. However, when the book was released in the U.S., the title was changed to *Harry Potter and the Sorcerer's Stone* because of the general belief that 1) American readers would not know what a philosopher's stone was; 2) that the word "philosopher" would be a turn-off . This second title does work within the context of the book. The stone in question was created and owned by a sorcerer. However, the act of retitling says a lot about how important titles are in making sure a book finds its audience.

I personally think that, for titles to do their best, they need to make sense. The publishers who decided to retitle this "Harry Potter" novel clearly had this in mind. If you know what a philosopher's stone is, really, this is a very intriguing title. If you don't, it's just misleading nonsense.

It also helps if titles within a series indicate they are part of a series. Sometimes, as with the Melina Marchetta books, structure is enough to show the connection. Sometimes a repeated word helps: Harry Potter and.... Sometimes a series title catches on, as with Robert Jordan's "Wheel of Time." More often though, the series tends to be referred to by the title of the first book. *Game of Thrones* is not the series title. That's "The Song of Ice and Fire."

Of course, the author does not always have control of the title. I learned this the hard way when some anonymous higher-up at Avon Books decided that the sequel to *Changer* could not be *Changer's Daughter*. After working through a long list of possible alternatives, my editor and I finally arrived at *Legends Walking*.

However, to this day, I encounter people who say, "You mean there's a sequel to *Changer*? I never realized it!" That's why, despite possible confusion, I gave *Legends Walking* back its original title when I re-released it as an e-book and POD.

The series title for my "Firekeeper Saga" never caught on. Even at Tor Books, the series tended to be referred to as "the wolf books." Therefore, imagine the confusion when the third book came out with a title that didn't have "wolf" in it. *The Dragon of Despair* was my working title for the manuscript, but I always assumed we'd come up with another title – one with "wolf" in it.

However, some anonymous person at Tor told my editor, "Oh, no! We like that. Books with 'dragon' in the title sell well." Maybe so, but when *The Dragon of Despair* was released, Tor had several other "dragon" books in the catalog… I think that probably only led to confusion.

So when you've finished your novel or short story and are revising it, don't forget to look at the title. It's the first part of the book anyone will see. Make certain it does your work – and your vision for the work – credit.

Car Crash or Culmination?

A while back, my friend, Tori asked if I'd explain why I frequently say that I can't tell whether a book or anime is "good" until I reach the end. I had to think about why for a while, but I finally came up with a way to explain this fairly complicated thought process.

Wanderings on Writing

(As an aside, I should note that I have different criteria for novels and visual media. Anime in particular often has a long story to tell, but does so in small chunks. Therefore, while I will look at novels as individual volumes, even if they are part of a larger series, I look at anime and some television as if each episode is a chapter in a longer work.)

I'm going to start by clarifying the question. What Tori was asking about were those stories that I enjoy enough to get involved with. So, this leaves out those stories that failed to hook me at the start or lost me early on. It only includes those that I'm enthusiastic enough about that I plan to finish. This means the stories already have the basics down (good characters, interesting plot elements, a well-defined setting). It also means that the subject matter suits my taste. I'm the first person to admit that there are plenty of really fine stories out there that simply don't work for me personally.

A great example of a book that I started with mixed feelings and ended up feeling enthusiastic about is Sue Grafton's *V is for Vengeance*. I'm a fan of the Kinsey Millhone novels. *V is for Vengeance* begins with a long prologue about which I had serious doubts. However, one of the reasons I've stayed with this series is that Grafton often shifts her storytelling format, something that has kept the series from becoming formulaic. So, long prologue or not, I kept with it.

At the end of the prologue, an event happened about which I felt strong doubts. To avoid spoilers, I'll just say that it had to do with the death of the young man who was central to the prologue. It wasn't so much that he died that troubled me, it was why he died. It didn't make sense.

Was Grafton slipping? Had her editors lost their minds? I'll admit, if this hadn't been the only audiobook I had available at that time, I might have quit. But, I've listened to all the other books in the series and I wanted to see what happened when Kinsey got on stage.

Jane Lindskold

Well, initially, I didn't feel a lot of hope. Kinsey's case involved a professional shoplifting ring. Eventually, there was a connection between the prologue and this plotline, but it seemed pretty thin – certainly not enough to justify that long, long prologue. Eventually, I put the prologue out of my head and concentrated on the story at hand. It had strong "grey" characters with complex motivations. There was lots of really cool information about how shoplifting, of all things, has become Big Business.

I can't say much more about the novel without providing too many spoilers but, as the book moved toward its final third, the prologue began to matter. By the book's conclusion I was bouncing up and down. Not only did the prologue matter, but better and better, the elements that I had thought were weak fit it. They weren't mistakes! They weren't sloppy writing! I was incredulously happy.

So, whereas when I started the book I would have said, "Pretty good, but I think Grafton's losing her touch or has become one of those writers who editors don't feel they can edit," now I would say: "Good novel. Clever. Interesting and surprisingly complex. I highly recommend."

I had a similar reaction to *The Black Prism* by Brent Weeks. Initially, I wanted to read it because Brent had been one of the Guests of Honor at Bubonicon and I had been intrigued by many of his comments during the Guest of Honor presentation. *The Black Prism* was a Very Fat Fantasy novel, however, and my reading time is very thin. I even considered looking for the book in audio, but some of Brent's (very funny) comments had been about the uneven quality of his audio book readers. I couldn't remember if this had been a book he had liked as presented in audio or not.

However, enough of the book interested me to keep me going. By the end, I could honestly say "I liked it. Interesting layered political problems. Complex characters. Gritty but not self-indulgently so. Creative magical system, well used and well intertwined into the plot." Will I read the next one? Yes. However, I'll probably wait until I can give it the time it deserves. This would be a perfect book for a long plane flight. Airport waiting time and flight time would seem a pleasure, not a burden.

Sadly, this is not always the case. I hate mentioning books that didn't work for me, but in this case I fear I must. One example is John Scalzi's popular novel, *Old Man's War*. I acquired it when it was a new release, so was unbiased by any press. I had met John Scalzi at a book fair and found him an intelligent person, so I was inclined to view the book with favor. I might even have started it on the plane on my way home.

Initially, I was very enthusiastic about *Old Man's War*. It had a good conceit, some interesting world-building, and characters I was interested in. I remember expressing my enthusiasm over the phone to my friend, Yvonne, ending, as I so often do, with "But I won't really know until I finish."

Sadly, by the time I finished, my enthusiasm had dimmed. The compelling question of how can society best use the wisdom and experience of older people whose bodies won't necessarily let them function at full capacity had vanished into action adventure heavily indebted to novels like Heinlein's *Starship Troopers*. (A novel which, by the by, I like.) The main character's difficult choices and ethical decisions were eliminated or diluted by a wealth of unlikely wish fulfillment.

Unlike, say, Terry England's excellent novel *Rewind*, which deals with similar questions without losing sight of them, even when the action becomes intense and the characters are in serious jeopardy, I felt that *Old Man's War* had the start of an excellent novel, and a car wreck of a conclusion.

I felt the same about the fan favorite TV series, *Firefly*. When Yvonne initially loaned me her set, thus allowing us to avoid the common excuse as to why the series failed ("They broadcast it erratically and out of order"), I was very enthusiastic. Good characters, complicated, intertwining plots, interesting setting. Strong individual episodes.

Some time in, though, I realized I was losing interest. Several of the plots were, as Jim put it, "They meet someone from the past who they're happy to see but turns out to be not the type of person they thought." The character development was wildly uneven, especially in the case of secondary characters. I began to see serious glitches in the world-building. I went from a potential fan to a "Well, I have no trouble seeing why this one didn't work."

So that's why I am likely to reserve my judgment as to whether or not a book or series works until I'm to the end. I might say, "I'm enjoying reading this or watching this." But it will be followed by, "I'll let you know how I feel when I'm done."

There are some novels or series that I like, even if they are in some way weak or disappointed me. However, these aren't the ones I recommend. If I do, I'm usually pretty realistic about admitting they have flaws but that – despite the flaws – there's something there I like.

Forgetting a Child

Back when my own fiction publications were few, I attended a Science Fiction convention at which artist Liz Danforth teased author Roger Zelazny about how, some years before at a different Science Fiction convention, her team had beaten his in a trivia game because Roger couldn't remember the name of one of his own characters.

For those of you who wonder, the character in question was Rosie from *Jack of Shadows*.

Wanderings on Writing

Rosie goes through a pretty tough time in that book. She plays a really important role, so, frankly, I was shocked. How could Roger have forgotten her?

Now here I am, many years later, author of more than twenty published novels and over sixty published short stories (and that doesn't count the ones I've written and haven't published). I've got to admit it. Especially in the case of secondary characters, yeah, I've probably forgotten a name or two. The character, no, but whether the name was Daisy or Rosie or Petunia, yeah... Probably.

Does this mean I don't care? Hardly. I love each and every one of those people, but the fact is that enough time has passed so I don't remember every one of them by name.

But then I'm not perfect in real life either. Here's an example. I like my sister Susan's in-laws a great deal. Even though we live far apart, we exchange Christmas cards and occasional notes. But every so often, I need to pause and think, "Nancy and... Ed! Right. Ed."

Does this mean I don't like Ed and Nancy? That I don't care? Hardly, but life goes on and names slip down behind others in the filing cabinet which is daily life.

However, there's another reason beyond just pure human forgetfulness that I sometimes forget when a book is coming out or exactly what some character's sister's name is. That reason is a strong, practical outgrowth of a rule that every writer – especially those who hope to someday be published – needs to remember.

Write it. Live it. Love it. Finish it. Send it out. And...

Forget it.

Yes. Forget it. Put it out of your mind. Start something else.

Jane Lindskold

But why? How? How can you possibly do that?

Well, the reality is that publishing is a slow, slow business. If you sit and wait for a reply on the fate of your "child" before starting something new, it's likely that you're going to do a whole lot more waiting than writing. Most writers prefer to be writing (a process in which I include editing, polishing, and, to a limited extent, researching).

Here's an example from my own experience. One January, a writer friend called to ask me if I wanted to work on a project with him. I said, "Maybe, sure. Send details." And my friend said, "I'll have X [the editor in question] get in touch with your agent." By mid-May, we still hadn't heard anything. In fact, it would be over a year before we'd even see a contract, longer before we'd start the books.

If I'd spent that time waiting, I would have spent a long time doing nothing. Instead, I did a lot of writing.

And, honestly, much as I love them, my books aren't my children. Children need constant care and reinforcement. Books don't. They don't care if you work on them or not. Children do.

My job as a writer is to move on – all the while hoping that, for those who encounter it, the story that was the focus of all my energy while I was writing it provokes thought, or inspiration, or even something as light as amusement to fill an idle hour.

Wanderings on Writing

Short Stories

The other day I found myself thinking about the strange dichotomy involved with me and short stories: I like to write short stories but I'm actually not much of a short story reader.

This was brought forcefully home to me when I was recommending Laini Taylor's collection *Lips Touch Three Times* to a friend. I heard myself saying, "I don't usually read short stories, but I really liked this. Of course, there are only three stories and they're long enough that they're more or less novellas..." Later in the same conversation, I mentioned that among my future projects I was looking forward to writing two short stories. I definitely heard the disconnect.

So, obviously, I need to think this through. First, there are definitely authors whose short stories I not only read but seek out. Roger Zelazny and Charles deLint both spring to mind. I bet if I thought longer, I could come up with others. There are those authors who are often better at a shorter length. I really like Walter Jon Williams' novels, but I think some of his strongest work is shorter. His novel *This Is Not a Game* is structured like two interconnected novellas and is all the better for it.

When I think back, I've actually read a lot of single-author short story collections and, in most cases, enjoyed them. So what's my problem?

Well, for one, I'm not a big fan of gimmick stories, no matter the length. I'm also not a big fan of inconclusive endings. Both of these are more likely to happen at shorter lengths, rather than longer. I have read too many short stories that are in reality descriptive vignettes. Someone has a clever idea or image and thinks that's all a story needs. It doesn't.

Fact is, a short story needs everything a novel does – and needs to present it within a smaller space, or at least with fewer words. (I leave the image because for me stories do seem to occupy a physical space. And I don't think that space is just a lump of pages.)

Roger Zelazny said – I'm not sure just where – that a short story should feel as if it was the final chapter of a novel. Maybe that's why I like his shorter works. He doesn't leave me hanging. I have tried to follow that advice with my own short stories and so am surprised how often, when I finish reading a story to a group, the immediate response is, "But what happened next?" Of course, I get that with my novels, too.

Short stories are also more often driven by ideas than by characters. I've written a lot of stories for theme anthologies. Sometimes the theme is very generalized – dragons, let's say, or angels – and sometimes it's more specific – alien pets or girls, guns, and monsters. I enjoy the challenge of trying to come up with a story that won't resemble anything else in the collection. That often means starting with a list of the usual – big dragons, wise dragons, nasty dragons – and vowing to avoid these.

Once I've made my list, I start musing about who the main character will be. For a short story, usually I try to keep the focus on one point-of-view character. Sometimes I'm in the mood to write about a certain type of person. Other times the theme dictates it. For the *Mother, Matron, Crone* anthology, for example, a female protagonist was pretty much a given.

Between these two, I arrive at my setting. Plot comes last of all. To avoid slipping into vignette-mode, I make sure I know what the conflict will be... even if I don't know the resolution. But I make certain there is a resolution. Just about the only people who like stories with indecisive endings are English professors – and that's because it gives something to discuss in the classroom.

Here's an example of the genesis of "Hunting the Unicorn," which appeared in *Courts of the Fey*, edited by Russell Davis.

Wanderings on Writing

As I noted above, especially when writing for a theme anthology, I do my best to make certain my contribution won't be generic. I started refreshing my familiarity with folklore related to the faerie courts – never a great trial for me. I also looked at Fantasy art, especially that of Brian Froud, Alan Lee, and the like – the people who are familiar enough with the source material to realize that the fey aren't nice.

There has been a lot – almost too much – contemporary Fantasy using the fey, so I decided my setting would be another world. Odd images floated in: dried rose buds, a black moon against a white sky. I scribbled them on a piece of paper, but didn't push too hard to see how they fit.

The heart of any good story is conflict. From my research, I'd seen how the motif of a hunt recurs over and over again in legends about the fey. What is more a creature of Fantasy than a unicorn? Okay then. A unicorn hunt.

I didn't want the usual hunt, though… What about a competition between the courts? Who would my champions be? I have a figure of a dark elf on the shelves behind my desk. I'd always felt there was a story to go with it. She became Blackrose of the Unseely Court. Her opponent became Sundeath of the Seely Court. I felt ready to let them ride forth…

Friday, I started writing. The story caught fire. I worked both Saturday and Sunday (not my usual practice, but time was tight and the story "hot"). By Sunday, when we left for our gaming date, I had a rough draft of something over seven thousand words.

Monday, I polished what I had (including reading the manuscript aloud to myself), printed a copy and handed it to Jim to proof. Tuesday night, Jim handed me the manuscript back with his comments. We also discussed the rather odd structure of the story and decided it worked. Wednesday, I made final changes, then sent the story off to Russell Davis. One of the nice things about electronic submissions is that I had an acceptance by the next day.

Most of my short story writing these days falls into the "by invitation" category – mostly because I'm pretty busy. I should note that an invitation to an anthology is *not* a sure sale. It may have a slightly higher chance of acceptance than a cold submission but, if your story doesn't work for the editor, rejection is quite possible. I've had it happen.

What if you're not writing by invitation? Actually, many of the tricks I mention above still work. Magazines have guidelines. Familiarize yourself with them. Consider reading the editor's column or – even better, since likely to be more current – blog or other social media. You may hear a lament that he has lots of contemporary Fantasy and would love a good adapted fairy tale. Or she has lots of space opera and would love some harder SF.

These can become challenges, similar to writing for an anthology. You can shift through your sheaf of ideas (most writers have more ideas than they have time to write) and see which fits.

Conversely, you might have an idea you're eager to write. Do so, but don't just submit at random. Familiarize yourself with markets – something that's easier than ever to do these days, since most have websites – and find the magazine or e-zine that seems like the best fit.

Short fiction can be very rewarding. Unlike a novel, which can take a year or more to write, a short story can be finished and edited within a week. It's a great way to polish your skills in developing plot, character, and setting.

Maybe you're reluctant to try short stories because you've heard a writer can't make a living doing short fiction. That's true... But there are very few full-time novelists, either. If that's your only reason for not trying short fiction, you probably need to take a look at why you're writing.

Wanderings on Writing

Changes Nothing

The other night, I dreamed I was talking with my former dissertation director, Dr. Philip Sicker, about a recently-published critical study of the poet W.H. Auden.

This led to a long discussion of the often quoted line "poetry changes nothing," from Auden's poem, "In Memory of W.B. Yeats."

Yeats, you see, believed poetry (and plays and fiction) could change things. Some people say he was right (after all, the Irish political landscape changed markedly in his lifetime, possibly in part because Yeats helped create a modern Irish cultural identity). Some people (and not Auden, by the by; read the whole poem) say poetry changes nothing.

My dissertation director and I (remember, this is a dream) went on to discuss whether or not literature does change anything. In the course of this, Dr. Sicker admitted that he'd tried some of my stuff, "but it just didn't work for me."

(I have no idea whether or not Dr. Sicker has ever read anything non-academic that I've written. Other than a few e-mails many years ago, we long ago fell out of touch.)

I said, "Well, I can see why. When I think back to the books we read in your Modern Literature classes, most of them were about people who didn't do much, certainly didn't change much. These books were basically about self-reflection. Sometimes, at the end, the person seemed to be moving toward change, but we rarely saw the change happen."

I went on, "The message in those books seemed to be 'You can't change anything.' No wonder they don't have much general appeal. No wonder young people turn to computer games or genre fiction for entertainment and inspiration. The implicit message in computer games and genre fiction (into which I'm lumping SF, Fantasy, Mysteries, and Thrillers) seems to be, 'If you're careful enough, if you plan, if you try and try again, you *can* change things.'"

Dr. Sicker nodded, but about that time (just before 5:00 a.m., dear lord) one of the cats decided she needed her ears rubbed. Abruptly awakened, I came out of the dream with a clear memory of the discussion and spent the next twenty minutes, until the alarm went off, thinking about it.

"Poetry doesn't change anything."

I just don't see it. Literature – in which I'm now lumping both "literary" and "popular" materials – has changed so many things, on so many levels for me, has introduced new ideas, has upset me or delighted me. Even those much maligned computer games have taught me things: patience, attention to detail, the value of cooperation.

Does it matter if the changes a story affects are on a small scale? Not really. After all, isn't that the implicit message in all those introspective literary fiction novels – that the smallest scale matters just as much as the largest?

I know some people write with an agenda, with a direct desire to try to change things. I'll admit, I don't. I write to tell a story, to go somewhere only that story can take me. From comments I've had from readers here and there over the years I've been writing, sometimes my writings have been a gateway into a change of life or at least a broadening of thought.

That's pretty darn cool.

Battling Against Distraction

These days, I'm lucky enough to be a full-time writer. However, when I started writing, that wasn't the case. Looking back, I see that habits and skills I cultivated at the beginning of my career continue to shape how I write today.

I started seriously applying myself to writing fiction immediately after I finished graduate school, even as I worked several part-time jobs, searched for a full-time post, and dealt with the usual demands of daily life. Then and there, I made three decisions. These basic choices remain the keynotes of my writing habits to this day.

1) *Writing Gets Priority*. This may sound simple, but it's actually very hard. Life seems to nibble away at writing time. For almost all my adult life, I've been in a serious relationship. I've owned and/or maintained my own home. I've always supported myself. No kids, but pets, gardens, gaming... I love to read. All huge time-eaters.

But no matter how drawn I am to these other things, I write. When I had another full-time job, I wrote seven days a week. Now that writing is my full-time job, I write five. This holds even when I have a "working weekend" doing book events or conventions.

2) *Avoid Boxes At All Costs*. I put this decision second only because I had to be serious about wanting to write before it could come into play. However, in many ways this is my creed.

There are many accounts of the curious rituals writers create for themselves. This writer can only write in complete privacy. That writer must have a certain drink or food. Another one has to wear certain "writing" or "lucky" clothes.

I resolved that my ritual would be no ritual. Privacy would need to go out the window. At the start, I lived in a small apartment with another person. Even when I had a larger place, much of my time was spent on a college campus. I shared my office. Students wandered in and out. So did my highly interesting colleagues.

Therefore, my "room of one's own" would need to be between my own ears.

The same ruthlessness had to be applied to the question of equipment. When I was finishing grad school, the hot new PC was the IBM 286. Bulky. Immobile. Expensive.

I touched-typed easily and quickly, but nevertheless I realized that the machine was a chain. I decided to pursue fiction writing longhand. Sometimes I simply carried a folded sheet of paper in my pocket. Most of the time, I managed to keep my current project on a clipboard along with my notes for whatever classes I was teaching.

Because of these two decisions, I wrote everywhere and every day. My first five novels were written longhand. So were hosts of short stories. I wrote while my students took quizzes. I wrote while waiting for appointments. I wrote when my gaming group met and my character was "off-stage." Memorably, I wrote an entire short story in a faculty meeting. ("Relief," published in the anthology *Heaven Sent*).

Most importantly, I wrote.

Wanderings on Writing

Sure, I had to retype those longhand manuscripts, but this was a good thing. Retyping forced me to carefully consider each word. I did a lot of revising as I retyped.

Time of day is the other big quirk by which writers trap themselves. I've known writers who need to write first thing or they won't "get into it." I've known writers who can only write at night when the world is quiet. I've known writers who can only write when their routine chores are completed and they feel they now "have time."

Often these writers adopted these habits for all the best reasons in the world, but what started as a good thing became a trap. I decided that no time would be my time. The reverse of this is that, for me, all time can be writing time.

Makes all the difference in the world.

3) *Be Flexible About Goals*. This is a two-parter, really. The other half is "But Have Goals."

When I started seriously addressing myself to writing, I had the good fortune to also be involved in an on-going correspondence (via snail mail) with author Roger Zelazny.

In one letter, Roger mentioned almost as an aside that three or four times a day he'd sit down and write three or four sentences. Sometimes the piece he was working on would catch fire and he'd find himself writing a lot more. Sometimes he'd just get those few sentences.

He commented that he never failed to be amazed how even just a few sentences a day could somehow turn into a finished piece. Roger also mentioned that, no matter how well the writing had gone the day before, he never gave himself a "break" because of that. The next day, he started with a fresh quota.

Jane Lindskold

Well, I'll admit I was somewhat indignant when I first read this. When was I (who was teaching five courses, sometimes five preps) going to find three or four times a day to write anything?

Then a little demon whispered in my ear: "Three or four multiplied by three or four is twelve."

Twelve. Twelve sentences, once a day. Surely I could manage that much. Twelve substantial sentences, of course, not just a "yes/ no" conversation.

Suddenly, indignation vanished. I felt eager and excited. I felt even more eager and excited when I realized that this tactic was working. I wrote short stories. Eventually, I wrote my first novel, then another. And more short stories.

I never let any other form of writing take over my quota. My non-fiction writing, of which I did a considerable amount, was done on the side. So was writing related to my teaching.

As Roger had said, sometimes those twelve sentences were enough to make my imagination take hold. I'd write a lot more, sometimes until my hand cramped and I was writing in a weird shorthand.

But I wrote.

When I began writing full-time, I adapted this goal. Early in a project, my goal is still just getting something on paper. Later, I expand that and try for five pages a day. Toward the end of a novel, when I'm eager to find out what's going to happen, I'm back to those days when my hands are cramping and my back is stiff, even when I shift chairs at my computer.

I suppose that this setting of production goals is a violation of my "no boxes" rule but, on the other hand, if I kept to that, then it would be a box of its own, wouldn't it?

Dealing with Deadlines... Or Not

One day, my friend Michael Wester asked, "Do authors work better under deadlines?"

I guess the first thing I'd better say is that I have no idea what "authors" do about anything. I only know what this one author does. Writers are more different than most people who share a common professional title. About the only thing they share in common is a desire to use words to create something. I say "desire" very specifically.

I've known an awful lot of people who refer to themselves as "writers" or "authors" who have never professionally published. Do I have a problem with this? Not at all. You don't need to have your work shown in a gallery to be considered a painter or sculptor. I do have a bit of a problem, however, with people who refer to themselves as "writers," yet who seem to spend a whole lot more time talking about writing than actually putting words down.

But that's another topic... Or maybe it isn't. I think that a writer needs to actually write – not to talk about writing – to be a writer.

And this brings me back to Michael's question: "Do authors work better under deadlines?"

I don't... Or rather, I don't need someone else to impose a deadline for me to write. If I have a contractual deadline, I usually do a bit of math and work out how much I need to write in a given month to meet it. In addition, I factor in time for me to read through the manuscript in full, beginning to end, red pencil the hell out of it, and make the corrections. Another element I work in is time for Jim to read the manuscript.

I take a look at my calendar and try to anticipate periods when it may be difficult to find time to write as much as I'd like – holidays, or upcoming trips, or other projects (for example, the time I will need to review a copyedited manuscript or page proofs on a book that's already in production).

When I don't have a deadline, as happens from time to time, I still tend to impose deadlines on myself – and meet them. I've written several novels that way, including *Through Wolf's Eyes*. I had written a proposal for my agent to shop around. Then one day it hit me.

I said to Jim:" I want to write this book no matter what, so I'll just write it. If Kay sells it based on the proposal, all well and good. If she doesn't, then she'll have a complete manuscript to shop around. And I'll have written the book I want to write."

Eventually, it was the full manuscript that sold. The nice thing was that I was then in a position to start the sequel as soon as it was under contract. *Wolf's Head, Wolf's Heart* was completed before *Through Wolf's Eyes* was released.

In fact, in my relatively long career as a writer of novels and short stories, I have missed only one contractual deadline. That was when my father died. Since I had to make several trips back and forth to Denver, I asked for (and was given with great compassion) an extension. I managed to be only six weeks late.

So do authors work better under deadlines? I guess my answer would be that this one does, but she prefers to inflict deadlines on herself.

Wanderings on Writing

Handstands in the Air

One year at the State Fair, we caught a performance by the Yang-dong Chinese Acrobatic Troupe.

In the span of about twenty-five minutes, we saw pole-climbing (and some fascinating controlled falls), hoop diving, astonishing leaps and bounces performed without benefit of a trampoline, an amazing contortionist, and a charming and dexterous woman who spun various lightweight objects (such as a paper umbrella) on her feet.

The troupe's coach took the stage to give an awesome demonstration that involved high-speed twirling of a wide-blade trident. This he whirled not only between his hands, but up and down his arms and over his back. This was an impressive enough display of controlled dexterity when he did his first set, but when, for the second round, both ends of the trident were set on fire, it was really amazing.

To make all of these performances more interesting, monsoon season was upon us. Gusty pre-thunderstorm winds meant that props often had their own idea where they should be heading. This was hard enough on the hoop divers and the contortionist (part of her performance involved five lighted candelabras). However, several times the winds removed the umbrella the young woman was twirling on her feet right off the stage.

Even so, for all of these, the winds were an inconvenience. The finale was a routine that the winds made not only challenging, but possibly dangerous. Those of you who have seen Chinese acrobats are probably familiar with some version of this routine. An acrobat, in this case a young woman, comes forth carrying a square-built chair and places it on the stage. Then she gets up on the seat and does handstands of various sorts.

The act becomes thrilling when an assistant brings out another chair. This one is set on top of the one below, upside down, so that the back of the upper chair rests on the seat of the lower chair. Now the young woman mounts to the upper reaches of this unfastened platform and does more handstands and the like.

This continues through a third chair, a fourth, a fifth, with the woman mounting about three feet higher each time. Jim and I were sitting in the center section, right in front of the stage and I am not exaggerating when I say that we could see the chairs swaying slightly when the winds hit. If the tower had gone down, the chairs and the acrobat would have been in our laps.

However, despite occasionally stopping for a moment when the winds were particularly strong, the young lady persisted. When she had built a tower five chairs high, a sixth one was lifted up to her. Not satisfied to repeat the routine she had done on the lower tiers, she braced this last chair at various angles and struck increasingly daring poses.

Please remember, the acrobat is not in a theater with safety nets beneath her, but on an outdoor stage amid gusty winds, winds that must have been augmented by the thunderous applause and shouts of appreciation from the audience below. The acrobat did have three spotters, but had she come down, they all would have been dodging chairs as they hoped to arrest her fall.

But she didn't fall. She finished her final twist, then, chair by chair, she dismounted, taking her bows with a beaming smile.

Now, as I already said, this routine is something of a classic. Even I, who have not seen that many Chinese acrobatic performances, have seen it before. Thinking about the act afterwards, I found myself wondering. When does something become a classic as opposed to "tried and true" or, far worse, "hackneyed," "old hat," and "clichéd"? Does something cease to be of value simply because you've seen it before?

Certainly, this was not the case for this tower of chairs routine. I'd be happy to watch it again – with or without high winds – many, many times again. Skill is skill. Talent is talent, at least in athletic performances.

However, writers (and others in the creative arts) face a different challenge. For writers (and the rest), often it is not enough to do the classic well. There is a craving for novelty – especially on the part of reviewers and editors. They want to see something new. Sometimes I'm not sure that this "new" thing needs to be particularly good. On the other hand, there are readers who want nothing new at all.

I once had my hair cut by a young woman who, when she learned that I wrote for a living and even wrote Fantasy, was very excited. She told me that she read Fantasy. She read Terry Brooks. When she had read whatever he had that was out and new, she went back and re-read old Terry Brooks novels. Apparently, that was all she read.

Now, I admit, this is an extreme example. However, as the writer, I definitely have seen both sides of the issue. For every fan letter I get expressing enthusiasm about a new project, I get two asking when I'm going to write a new Firekeeper novel, or a new Changer novel, or a fourth "Breaking the Wall" novel or maybe a sequel to my novels *Child of a Rainless Year* or *The Buried Pyramid*.

Sometimes, fans of a particular series will not hesitate to tell me they cannot stand the other works I have done, as if this will encourage me to fulfill their request. Even short stories can trigger this "more, but the same" response. When I read my short story "Hunting the Unicorn" at Bubonicon, the first question was, "What happens next?"

Yet reviewers and editors are the first to say "ho, hum" to the classic. Sometimes, more puzzling, especially from those on the buying end, a writer hears, "Can you give us more of the same but different, please?"

So what choice should writers who are hoping to break in to the business make? Should they follow the current hot trend or write whatever they feel like?

Remember this. By the time you finish your book, the market will probably be saturated with the current hot trend. So, unless you really love wizard school stories or vampire romances or ugly medieval wars or space opera, don't waste your time.

Now, if you really love whatever the trend is, don't feel you must not write your take on it. Your passion may very well give your work a special flavor. However, don't feel you can file the serial numbers off someone else's work, change a few names, and have a sellable product.

Passion for your topic really matters. A great example of this is George R.R. Martin's "Game of Thrones" series. George did not invent anything new here. There have been epic fantasies for a long time. There have even been fantasies with nasty characters and lots of sex. What George brought to his topic was a life-long love for tales of knights in shining armor, daring deeds, and mystic threats. Where he's derivative, it's the derivation of homage, not mere imitation.

Editors are often more attracted than the average reader to something fresh and new. Something riding the tail end of a burning-out trend isn't going to interest them. They're more likely to take something derivative from an established name. A new reader needs to offer something that shows freshness or passion or, preferably, a bit of both.

Make your tower of chairs and dance on it. It may be an old trick, but if you give it your own flair, then you'll wow your audience.

Wanderings on Writing

Writer's Block

A friend asked me once, "You always hear about 'writer's block.' What do you do when you get 'stuck' creatively? Does taking a break get you back on track? How often does it happen? What's the worst you've ever experienced?"

Okay. Let's start with defining writer's block, because there are a lot of misunderstandings about what it is. Writer's block is completely different from being "stuck" – that is, uncertain about where to take a story or how to resolve a problem in the plot or how to develop a character. Pauses in the development of a story are something that every writer faces. I talked some about how I deal with these hitches in the writing process in "Walking Away From It."

Writer's block is completely different. Writer's block is a crippling inability to write. I'm a disciplined and determined writer. If I hadn't encountered writer's block personally, I think I'd be inclined to believe that when people say they're blocked, they just making an excuse not to write. However, I've had it. I know it's real. And really terrible.

Here's what happened... Many years ago, when I was teaching at Lynchburg College in Virginia, I also was working hard on getting established as a fiction writer. Every day, no matter how demanding my day job, I'd make time to write. When I finished a story and polished it, I'd send it out to one of the SF/F magazines. Then I'd put it out of my mind and start something new. When a story came back with a rejection, I'd go over it, then send it out again. (This was in the late 1980s or early 1990s, so neither disposable manuscripts nor electronic submissions and correspondence had become routine.)

There came a day when I had five short stories out. I was feeling hopeful that one of them would get published. I came home from work, unlocked the tiny mailbox in my apartment house entryway, and found every single story I'd sent out smashed into the box. Each had a form rejection. I'm not sure that anyone had even looked at them.

My gut lurched, but I didn't realize how hard that torrent of rejection had hit me until I sat down that evening to write. I'd been working on a story. I curled up with my pen and clipboard (I always wrote rough drafts long-hand) and my hand began to shake. I couldn't write a single word. The story had vanished. All I could envision was more rejection. Maybe the couple of stories I'd already sold had been flukes. Maybe I didn't have what it took.

I gave myself that night off and graded papers instead. The next night, I sat down to write. Again, I started shaking. Night after night, this went on. It was horrible. I could write letters. I could write material for my classes. I could write non-fiction. But writing a story was impossible.

(I've got to pause here. My heart's racing with remembered fear and pain.)

What saved me was that my desire to tell a story was stronger than my fear that no one but me would ever read it. I was teaching a course on mythology and one of my students asked, "Dr. Lindskold, I just don't get this Orpheus guy. What is it he does?"

I considered, then I said, "Well, Shannon, when you were a kid, did you ever hear the story of the Pied Piper of Hamlin? Orpheus was like that, except that it wasn't just children or rats that were charmed by his music, it was everything. Even rocks or trees would try to get closer to him when he began to sing."

Wanderings on Writing

And as the discussion continued, as we moved on to the eventual tragedy of Orpheus's life, a small part of my brain that had been too long dormant came alive. "What if," it said, "Orpheus didn't die? What if he escaped the maenads? What if he somehow lived to become the Pied Piper?"

That night, I took out pen and paper for the first time in what felt like forever. I wasn't writing, I assured myself. I was just making a few notes. Every page I filled, I slid to the back of my clipboard unread, un-reviewed. After all, I wasn't writing. Eventually, I had more than the clip could hold. I put these in a folder and stuffed the folder on a shelf. I kept writing until I had the longest thing I'd ever written. Somewhere along the way, the block was beaten.

If this were a movie, I would then sell the novel immediately, win awards, and thumb my nose at those who had rejected me. What happened in reality was that, even though this was a long piece, it wasn't long enough. When I sent it out, it got rejected. However, eventually I expanded it, adding a second part to the story. It would come out many years later as my third published novel, *The Pipes of Orpheus*.

I hope that answers the questions. To me, writer's block is different than simply getting "stuck." Since it has its roots in something more complex, simply taking a break won't be enough to fix the problem. It's called "writer's *block*," not "writer's stuck," for a reason, and being blocked is hell for a writer. To answer the one remaining question, it's only happened once to me. I hope and pray it never happens again.

Jane Lindskold

At a Loss...

As anyone knows who has ever stared at the wall in desperation trying to figure out what to write for some college essay assignment, formulating the idea is half or even three-quarters of the battle. Back then, I'd spend a considerable amount of time rendering all my various thoughts down to a simple, one sentence thesis statement. After that, the rest of the paper would flow easily.

The same can be true with fiction writing. Getting the idea, whether for the overall project or for the particular section one is working on, is the biggest challenge. Once you slip into your characters' heads, then the story toddles along quite nicely. Getting in there is the hard part.

By purest coincidence, over the last couple of months, I spoke with two professional writer friends who admitted that they were behind because they had assumed they could take on more work by scheduling themselves to write on Project One in the morning and Project Two in the afternoon. Both of these gentlemen – many time published, quite experienced authors – discovered that this was impossible. Once they were securely into one universe, their imaginations did not want to shift into the other.

Even worse, they discovered that the Morning/ Afternoon division of labor did not work, because even prolific writers seem to have only so much writing in them. When that writing has been expended, the Muse acts like a camel that has had the proverbial "last straw" loaded into her panniers. She folds her legs under herself, sits down, and refuses to get up until the unreasonable burden is removed.

So, how does a writer cope with this? One way is to do what I'm doing right now – start writing and see what comes out. I believe I've mentioned that when I can't seem to write anything, I make myself write at least twelve sentences.

Wanderings on Writing

This number evolved from a time when Roger Zelazny mentioned to me that he managed to sit down three or four times a day and write three to four sentences each time and that somehow this managed to turn into a considerable amount of finished prose – especially since when he had a really good day and wrote pages and pages, he didn't take the next day off, but went right back to that sitting down three to four times a day and writing three to four sentences.

Anyhow, I was teaching college then and was lucky if I could find time to work on fiction once a day, so I multiplied three to four times by three to four sentences and arrived at twelve. It worked. I wrote four novels and quite a number of short stories while teaching college fulltime, by dedicating time to getting those twelve sentences on paper. (And I was teaching English, so I was also spending a huge amount of time reading and grading essays. This is not an inspirational activity, I assure you.)

Nonetheless, even with the best will and finest discipline in the universe, it seems that the Muse is only willing to let a writer come up with so much prose in a day. How much varies from writer to writer. However, I firmly believe that with a strict exercise regime, the Muse can be convinced to give a little bit more, just as a runner or swimmer can go from doing one or two laps to three or four, on and on, until a whole mile is reached.

But the training takes patience and quite a bit of understanding of one's own temperament. This is one reason I only write one Wednesday Wandering a week. Often on the day that I write it, my creative well is dry for the day. My Muse turns camel. Even if I remind her that we weren't writing fiction, just a nice, bouncy little essay, she says, "Hah! You can't fool me." Sometimes she's kinder and will accept a division between fiction and non-fiction.

Tempting the Muse works best for me if the fiction piece is already underway, especially if I stopped in the middle of a particularly juicy scene, so that the Muse is eager to show off how we're going to get our characters out of whatever predicament they're in at that moment.

Jane Lindskold

Sometimes even that isn't enough.

So, my advice if you're stuck? Write. Even when you don't think you have anything to write about, write. You just might (as I have myself today) surprise yourself!

Welcome to My Subconscious

When someone asks me, "Where do you get your ideas?", I'm handicapped, because I'm a subconscious plotter. I can talk about my lifelong love of mythology or of wolves, but usually I can't trace precisely where a book originated.

Some writers can do this and I admire them. I once had the chance to ask Tim Powers why he wrote, some twenty years later, a sequel to his novel *The Stress of Her Regard*. Tim had a neat, tidy, and humorous explanation for the circumstances that led to the writing of *Hide Me Among the Graves*. I only wish I could be so lucid.

Here's an example of how my subconscious works, taken not from my life as a writer, but from my life as a role-playing gamer.

Back in the mid-nineties, Jim and I were involved in a role-playing game in which the players were all members of an FBI serial killer detection unit. (Yeah... Get a bunch of SF/F writers together – in addition to me, Walter Jon Williams, Pati Nagle, and Melinda Snodgrass were all involved – and the impulse arises to play cops and robbers.)

Wanderings on Writing

Anyhow, our team was assigned to find a suspected serial killer. There were a lot of murders, but no one could figure out what – if any – pattern the killings followed. Making matters worse, we couldn't be sure which of the many unsolved case files that were handed over to us applied to our problem and which might be unrelated.

I mean, how might the murders of four prostitutes be related to the hanging in a public park of actor Danny Bonaduce (of Partridge Family fame)? Did the murder of five people and the removal of their wedding rings have anything to do with our serial killer or was the source of those killings related to some aspect in the lives of the people involved? That night after the game ended, Jim and I went home more puzzled than ever. By the time we'd settled the animals and gone to bed, it was very late indeed. Then, about four a.m., nature awoke me.

As I was pulling my weary carcass out of bed, I realized my sleeping brain had been working through the elements of the various crimes, shifting and sorting, weighing and discarding. All these years later, I can't remember the details of all the crimes (especially the red herrings), but I do remember most of the key ones.

Danny Partridge found dead in a park, an apparent suicide, hanging from a tree. Three French priests. Five wedding rings. Gold rings. Four prostitutes. Call girls. Calling Birds. Four calling birds.

My body wanted to go to sleep. My brain kept swirling odd bits and pieces around. Finally, I had it! The song "The Twelve Days of Christmas." The serial killer was working his way through The Twelve Days of Christmas! What was six? Six Geese a'laying.

We should check to see if there were any killings related to six geese a'laying. If there hadn't been, maybe we could figure out a likely target and set a trap of some sort for the killer!

Jane Lindskold

Suddenly, I was wide awake and wildly excited. I poked my drowsing spouse.

"Jim! Jim! I've got it! He's doing The Twelve Days of Christmas!"

Inarticulate mutterings into a pillow resolved into intelligent speech. "What? Who? He is? What?"

Feverishly, I explained, showing how with a little allowing for bad puns, the pattern was there. A partridge in a pear tree. Three French men, rather than three French hens. Four calling girls. Five golden rings. Jim agreed. He started settling back to sleep.

"I've got to call Melinda!"

"It's 4:30 in the morning. We didn't leave her house until after midnight."

"But I've got the answer. I've got to call Richard. He's the boss. He'll know what we should do next."

"No. You are not calling Melinda at four a.m."

"She gets up early to feed the horses…"

"Fine. Call then. Not at four a.m.…."

So I tossed and turned, at last getting up and making the phone call rather earlier than was strictly polite. Melinda responded with enthusiasm. Later, the game master would ask me, "What gave it away? I thought it would take at least to seven, even eight, before you all saw the pattern." I had to reply, "I don't know. I solved it in my sleep."

And that's how I write, too. Not necessarily in my sleep, but by trusting that the story is there, buried in my subconscious mind. Writing from the subconscious makes my characters very real to me. I can feel when a situation is right or wrong for them. It also means I'm not very good at workshopping because, often until a book is nearly done, I don't have the faintest idea where it's going.

Still... That's how it works for me... I do a lot of research, a lot of thinking, but ultimately the stories come out of the borderland between the land of waking and that of dreams.

Zink Makes Me Think

The artwork caught my eye first, a diorama featuring several miniature samurai helmets on an irregularly shaped platform hanging from a wall in a gallery in the Albuquerque Museum. When I went to read the title ("Spectacular Helmet" by Melissa Zink), the quotation included on the tag drove everything else out of my mind.

> *"It's like you're walking around with this enormous suitcase full of magic and you are never allowed to open it, because the rules say that the things in that suitcase are not worthy of artistic consideration. Worlds, child-hood memories, pretend, fantasy, archaeology — all that. And so, until I could open that suitcase, I really didn't have anything to work with. It was like trying to paint with your hands tied behind your back."* Melissa Zink.

These words thrilled and excited me – so much so that they brought tears to my eyes. Although up to that time, Jim, our friend Michael Wester, and I had been having a lively discussion of both the art we were viewing and whether or not we thought the captions and titles did the art justice, I found myself reluctant to comment. Then Michael said something like, "That's a really amazing statement."

I was astonished. I'd thought the words meant so much to me because I was a writer who had her own "enormous suitcase full of magic" and regularly delved into it – despite my awareness that, in the academic world in which I did my education, "the things in that suitcase are not worthy of artistic consideration." However, here was Michael – a professional mathematician – finding himself moved by those words as well. Now, admittedly, Michael is an eclectic personality, interested in far more than mathematics, but his statement made me wonder how many of us carry around private suitcases that we're apprehensive about opening in public lest the contents be deemed unworthy of consideration.

I decided then and there that we needed a copy of the quotation. I was about to hand copy it, but one of the guys suggested that maybe we could photograph it. Since photography was forbidden in the museum, I hurried off and found the gallery guard. My words tumbling over each other, I explained what we'd like to do. He smiled, genuinely delighted by our enthusiasm and said, "You like Zink? Let me come over and you can take your picture."

We did. Later Jim transcribed the quote and I sent Michael a copy. That might have been the end of it except that, a week or so later, when I was at the library researching something else entirely, I came across a book about Melissa Zink's art. It was titled *The Language of Enchantment* and had been written by Hollis Walker, a gallery owner who had loved Melissa Zink's work since she first encountered it in 1978 and who had represented Zink since 1993.

As I read Walker's introduction, once again I was chilled down to my soul: "The principle source of Zink's inspiration has been books. She's passionate about them, down to the way they smell, everything that contributes to what she thinks of as the 'book experience,' and the expression of that passion has been the central concern of her career."

I turned the pages, looking at the photographs of Zink's art, feeling rather like Alice gazing through the looking glass into a world that belonged to someone else but nonetheless was deeply familiar. I loved the narrative dioramas from the series "The (almost) True-To-Life Adventures of Gypsy Dog and Hattie Macwilliam in Darkest Artland." Later in her career, Zink moved from these dioramas to "wall-hung pieces with two-dimensional aspects" such as the piece that had caught my eye in the Albuquerque Museum. Later still, she tightened her focus down to letters and words, creating unique alphabets or illustrating a single word. No matter how abstract the work became, the sense of story remained.

Most of Zink's works were small but, when she tried her hand at works on a larger scale, the written word remained her inspiration. Her "Guardians" were "The Minister of Words," "Chamberlain of Letters," and "Book Warden." Walker's book showed Zink impishly peeking out from behind the three tall bronze figures, their androgynous heads set atop flattened bodies made from text.

Looking at Zink's work, I found myself understanding afresh why books I can hold in my hand mean so much to me. Her generosity in sharing her suitcase of ideas brought home to me how a book, a word, a letter, are all more than merely mediums for the translation of ideas. The written word, the printed word, the smell of paper and ink, take me somewhere. There is a magical experience in the act of reading, what Zink herself called "a trance state."

I don't think it's coincidental that for many people this sense of magic is tied to the physical book. A good friend of mine was given an e-book device for Christmas. A dedicated reader, she found this quick and easy way of getting stories to read – without even having to leave the house or wait for something to be shipped to her – surprisingly addictive. However, she's also commented that, if she really loves a book, she buys a physical copy. Holding the book makes it somehow more "hers."

Makes me think…

Homage or Hack Work?

Every reader has quirks. Some people don't like graphic sex scenes. Some people find detailed combat dull. Some people don't care how many human characters are killed in the course of a novel, but kill an animal – especially a cat or dog – and the author will be in, well, the dog house...

My quirk is a little different. I really dislike books that are recognizably based on someone else's novels or characters or named settings.

By this I don't mean collaborations, where the original author is part of the project. I've done several of these, *Fire Season* and *Treecat Wars* with David Weber, which use Weber's character, Stephanie Harrington. I've also written several "Honorverse" novellas at Weber's invitation. I've written a Berserker story with Fred Saberhagen and expanded the history of his *Mask of the Sun* (in the anthology, *Golden Reflections*). I wrote a story for the Jack Williamson tribute anthology, *The Williamson Effect*. I also had my go at Larry Niven's Known Space in a Man/Kzin War anthology.

What pushes my buttons to the point that I won't even pick up the novel are those books that are based around highly recognizable fictional characters: the many refurbishments of Sherlock Holmes, the increasingly numerous expansions of cast of Jane Austin's *Pride and Prejudice*, *The Wizard of Oz* revamped, *Jane Eyre*...

As an author, I did step over this line twice. Once, when invited to do a story for the anthology *Fantastic Alice*. However, even then I was very careful to tell my tale "outside" of the Alice in Wonderland canon, not just recycle Alice and the Queen of Hearts or the Walrus and the Carpenter... My story was from the point of view of the Dormouse and tells what happens when he's in the teapot. To tell the truth, if asked today, when the market seems increasingly glutted with novels based on other people's works, I would probably decline. The other time was in a Lovecraft anthology. Since Lovecraft opened up the gates to his uncanny realms during his own lifetime, I didn't feel I was abusing his property.

So why does fiction – especially novels – based on other writer's works bother me so much, especially since I'm not bothered by stories that use mythology or folklore as a foundation?

Basically, it's because while mythology and folklore belong to a culture – to a group of people who share an ethnic or religious background – fictional characters belong to that one author. I can't help but feel as if these works – especially ongoing series that don't even bother to file off the serial numbers – are less affectionate homages, more attempts to capitalize on someone else's works. Even when it's legal – as with characters whose original novels have entered the public domain – I just don't care for it.

The *Iliad* and *Odyssey* or *Aeneid* have named authors (in these cases Homer and Virgil), but still fall into the "mythology and folklore" category for me, since it's quite likely that the "authors" were less authors and more compilers of long-standing oral traditions. That is, Homer and Virgil took material that was already being told around the fireside and arranged it into what has become the "official" version.

Jane Lindskold

Once, when we were working on a Tangent, Alan Robson mentioned how certain fictional elements have become part of our modern "mythology": Dracula, Tarzan, Sherlock Holmes, Frankenstein, Jack the Ripper (a historical figure, but one who has been fictionalized so often that most people couldn't sort apart the fictional elements from the non-fictional) and others. While in the context of our discussion, I saw his point, still...

Frankly, I don't read the stuff. If you want me as a reader, don't ride into the literary arena on someone else's coattails. Give me your own people and places. I'm much more likely to give your works a try.

Fan Fiction

In "Homage or Hack Work?", I wrote about my dislike of fiction based on someone else's fictional characters or universe. I don't know why, but I never anticipated that the subject of "fan fiction" would come up in response.

How do I define fan fiction and how is it different from the type of novels I discussed last week?

The biggest difference is that fan fiction is often written about works that are actively owned by someone else, rather than being in the public domain. Sherlock Holmes is (mostly) in the public domain. So is Jane Austen. So is *The Wizard of Oz*. And *Jane Eyre*. Even though a single unique author wrote the work, that author's copyright has expired and the work is now open for use by the greater public.

Wanderings on Writing

What takes a work out of copyright? Time. Pretty much nothing else. No. It doesn't matter if the work is no longer in print. That doesn't mean it's in the public domain, any more than the fact that you're not wearing a certain pair of shoes means that someone else can take them from your closet and wear them.

Always be careful about assuming a work is no longer protected by copyright. Copyrights can be renewed. Translations are copyrighted separately than the work from which they were translated. Sometimes (as in the case of the poet Emily Dickinson), a work may be published after the author's death and so the copyright has nothing to do with the life span of the original author, but rather with the date of first publication of the particular piece.

Fan fiction has a long tradition. However, only with the advent of the Internet could writers of fan fiction easily disseminate their work to a large audience. Before that, availability was usually limited by the number of copies the fan author could produce. The mimeographed fanzine was later succeeded by the photocopier, but both of these involved some expense and – in many cases – a considerable outlay for postage.

The Internet has changed all of that. Now fan writers can publish their take on Harry Potter or *Game of Thrones* or whatever takes their fancy at the push of a button or two. Moreover, instead of being available to a few hundred people, the work is available to the world. (Available doesn't mean read by, just available.)

Is this really publishing? Fan writers may not think so – after all, no one has paid them for their work. However, according to a prominent intellectual properties attorney who I consulted before writing this, yes, posting something on the Internet counts as publishing, even if no money changes hands. Therefore, it is a violation of the original author's copyrighted material.

I asked several writers how they felt about fan fiction based on their work. Most said that, although they were flattered, even if they did not actively attempt to "shut down" the writer, they would prefer that people didn't write fan fiction and publish it on the Internet. Many stated that they do not read fan fiction based on their own works, lest at some future time there be a potential conflict.

How do I feel? Pretty much the same. I've been repeatedly approached by fans of my works asking if they can write fan fiction or a script or do a comic book based on my works. My answer is always the same... What you do in private, to stimulate your personal creativity, is your own business. However, if you really love my worlds and characters, please don't attempt to profit from them, even if the only profit is a boost to your ego.

(I should note that the intellectual property attorney I consulted said that "commercial gain" can be widely interpreted by courts. Simply driving a lot of traffic to your website can be construed as commercial gain, especially if the website or blog runs advertisements or in any way generates income for anyone at all.)

If you do think you have written a saleable screenplay or script, then talk to my agent. Don't show it to me. I won't read it. Worse. I really can't read it without setting myself up for a potentially ugly situation down the road.

Ugly? Here's what I mean...

About the time I was starting my career, a Very Famous Science Fiction Writer (VFSFW) who shall remain nameless was sued by someone who claimed that the VFSFW had stolen his idea. As evidence, the person bringing the suit produced a short story and a letter from the VFSFW commenting on that short story. A jury who knew nothing about SF – including how many shared concepts there are (things like faster-than-light travel or space colonies or anti-gravity) decided that VFSFW had taken advantage of the poor new writer. Damages were, reportedly, considerable.

Wanderings on Writing

This isn't precisely the same situation as fan fiction. However, fan fiction holds the potential for the same sort of situation – or even worse. After all, the characters, setting, and even elements of plot may be the same. So, sadly, professional writers are forced to protect themselves by walking a tightrope between awareness and ignorance. The situation becomes even worse with trademarked material, but I'm not going into that.

Yes. There is such a thing as fair use, but fan fiction rarely stays within those very limited parameters, so I'm not going into that particular issue here. Sometimes even a very limited reference to another writer's work or setting – such as Walter Jon William's reference to "Damnation Alley" in his novel *Hardwired* – can make a publisher insist on permission from the original author before they will publish the work in question.

I'm not immune to the appeal of writing fan fiction. I've done my share – as has almost every writer I know. Some fan fiction is written because the writer has an idea about something the characters might have done but didn't. Another reason is that the fan fiction writer has come up with a story that will smooth out a perceived problem within the official storyline. Another common reason for writing fan fiction is because the series or book has ended, and the fan needs to fill the void.

Fan fiction can be a great way to write with "training wheels." (I have used this term for years and was amused when my fellow writer Steve Gould – author of *Jumper* and the recently published *Impulse* – used it in his response to my query.) After all, someone else has created the characters, the setting (including all the world-building – a thing that looks easy until you start doing it), and may have even provided the seed for the plot.

All the fan writer has to do is come up with the rest of the plot and maybe a supporting character or two. It's a great way to learn. But it's not a great way to publish.

Jane Lindskold

Works such as those based on Sherlock Holmes or *The Wizard of Oz*, or sequels approved by an author's estate, or even collaborative works, may give the uninformed writer the idea that anything published is up for grabs. It isn't. Keep your fan fiction to yourself and a small group of friends. Everyone will be happier for it.

Pausing for Poetry

I've been reading a lot of poetry lately.

There was a time in my life that poetry had a daily place. I was an undergraduate English major, and then continued studying English literature through a Ph.D. After that, I taught English at the college level. That involved reading a lot of poetry, too.

I never really stopped reading poetry, but the automatic inclusion of poetry into my daily routine began to be, well, less automatic. There were periods that the desire to read poetry rose in intensity. There was the time I read Jim all the selections from T.S. Eliot's *Book of Practical Cats*, one an evening. That led me to re-reading a lot of Eliot's more "serious" verse and some of his verse drama.

Then Jim got into "Cowboy Poetry" – a rather specialized form of verse. One of the qualifications to be a "genuine" cowboy poet is to have worked as a cowboy. Jim's co-worker Jeff Boyer is an official cowboy poet, some compensation for the aches and pains he has as a heritage of those rough days in the saddle. Jim started

Wanderings on Writing

by reading Jeff's offerings, then went on to other writers of the form. Cowboy poetry isn't bad, especially if you like rhyming verse (we both do) that tells a story or joke.

Another time, I was asked to write a story for the Irish-themed anthology *Emerald Magic*, edited by Andrew M. Greeley. I decided to write a story featuring the poet W.B. Yeats and the lady he never stopped loving, Maud Gonne. "The Lady in Grey" didn't feature any poetry, as such, but it gave me an excuse to re-read a lot of Yeats's work. Then, as a means of keeping Yeats' language and cadence in my mind while I wrote, I listened over and over to a recording titled "Songs and Music from the Cuchulain Cycle" that had been given to me many years ago. Grand stuff. I think Yeats actually would have approved of the Celtic rock beat to which the "The Harlot and the Beggar Man" is set at the end. It's stirring, caustic stuff that fits his words perfectly.

So here I am, reading poetry again. I started as research, but this time the bug bit deep. I kept a tattered poetry anthology on my desk until the wind blew it apart. A couple times a day I'd opened it at random. Now, this anthology purports to contain "Immortal Poems of the English Language," so I guess I shouldn't be surprised, but I remain astonished how many of the pieces I read contain lines that remain in daily use – even by people who would swear they know nothing about poetry.

Poetry is a good reminder of how a few well-chosen words can say more than paragraphs. In fact, one definition of poetry I came across recently said that the art of writing poetry could be defined as finding the least possible number of words needed to get across an idea. Not bad...

Jane Lindskold

Life with a Writer

I thought I'd present you with a two-part look at life with a writer. In this piece I'm going to focus what life with a writer is like. In the following one, I'll focus on the question of what writers owe those with whom they live.

I feel pretty qualified to write about this because, in addition to having been a full-time writer since 1994, I've been seriously working on being a writer since I finished writing my doctoral dissertation in 1988.

Additionally, I've been on the other side of the equation. I lived with writer Roger Zelazny. Before that, we were avid and enthusiastic correspondents so, even before we were living under the same roof, I had a good idea of how he dealt with the demands both of being a writer and a member of a family. My husband, Jim Moore, is an archeologist. What you may not realize is that archeology – especially the type that Jim does – involves a lot of writing. So, in a sense, I'm still living with a writer.

Jim and I have done a lot of thinking about how to live happily with a writer. Here are a few things we've figured out, presented in a semi-logical order.

One: Writing involves more than writing.

A writer is writing even when fingers are not moving either pen or keys or anything at all. In fact, the times when a writer is staring at the wall, apparently doing nothing, or playing solitaire on the computer, or reading, may actually be when the writer is working very hard indeed.

So, the worst thing you can say to your writer at these times is, "Since you're not doing anything, could you..."

Really, you're likely to start fireworks.

Two: Life with a writer is not cool. In fact, it's excruciatingly boring.

Several writer friends have told variations on the following tale. They get into a relationship with someone, in part because that someone thinks that writing is "cool." Then, once the relationship is underway, the non-writer is shocked that the writer needs time to write...

Sounds stupid, but I've seen it happen a lot. Don't get into a relationship with a writer if you can't take that he or she is going to spend a lot of time with other people and traveling to other places. Even worse, those people and places don't exist, so all those rules in relationship guides about making yourself interested in your partner's life and interests simply don't apply.

Maybe your writer will want you to know every bit about a work in process. In that case, you're going to need to struggle against boredom and repetition. Maybe your writer won't want to share anything until the project is done, so you'll just get a lot of fragmentary comments.

My friend Sharon Weber has been known to say, "My husband has a mistress. Her name is Honor Harrington."

Three: Writers are very different from each other.

Seriously. Except for the fact that they all make up stories, most writers have little in common. Some are like me: they write a bit every day and end up with a book. Others are binge writers. They might not seem to do anything for weeks and then seem glued to their computer. Some can work a nine-to-five sort of schedule. Some need to work at night, when distractions are at a minimum. Some need to start first thing...

There is no one guidebook that will suit every writer. However, if you're going to live with a writer, you need to learn that particular writer's signals: when things are going well; when they're going horribly; when there is a real obstruction in the creative process, and when it's just a temporary stoppage.

I am very fond of a passage from Agatha Christie's autobiography where she talks about her recurring problems at the start of each novel. She also notes how her husband, Max, reacted. I recognized that reaction. It's very similar to how Jim reacts to me. I wonder if it has anything to do with both of them being archaeologists?

So, just as you'd learn the care and feeding of an exotic pet, you need to learn the care and feeding of your particular writer. He or she will appreciate it – and so will you, especially when you find yourself being praised for being such an important part of the creative process, even when you don't write a single word.

There's a reason that every book I've written since Jim and I have been together is dedicated, in all or in part, to him.

Four: Writers Need Stroking.

Why? Because, most of the time, they don't get any at all.

Really, this is true. Even the most famous of the famous – unless they decide to make a career out of being famous – spend a lot of time alone, working really hard at something that won't be seen by its intended audience until months or, more probably, years after it is concluded.

When writers do get attention, it's disproportionately small in regard to the work involved. A book may take a year to write, then another year going through various stages of production. When it finally comes out, there is an intense month or so of interest. Then, for maybe the next six months, there might be late reviews or interviews. After that, all anyone seems to care about is what's next.

Five: Writers have different times when they want to celebrate.

For me, the day that I finish a manuscript in rough – so that it has a beginning, middle, and end – is actually my day of greatest celebration. Jim has learned this and goes out of his way to share my pleasure. He knows perfectly well that I'm not done with the book, but he recognizes that for me this is a special time.

Jim also realizes that, for me, the release of a book is more a time for trepidation than celebration. That's when I need to worry about reviews, about giving interviews, about doing my best at book events. However, he reminds me about the good stuff – especially to take pleasure in the book's release – and so helps me keep my balance.

In between, when I'm just struggling to get words on the page, to keep up my enthusiasm in the face of very human doubt, Jim provides encouragement. I really value how often he asks, "How did the writing go today?" even when the sour look on my face promises a grumpy reply.

Okay... So that's a bit of a look at what it's like to live with a writer. In the next piece, I'll look at what writers can do to make living with a bundle of creativity a bit less maddening for their loved ones.

Jane Lindskold

What a Writer Owes

In "Life with a Writer," I took a look at living with writers with special emphasis on some of the oddities involved. This week, I want to take a look at what writers owe those who live with them. In my last piece, mostly for reasons of convenience, I presented matters as if to a writer's partner. In this piece, I'm going to expand a bit and include family and even friends.

One: So you're a writer. So what?

Writers are pretty funny creatures in that they expect the people around them to take an interest in what they produce. They want their partners to read what they write, to comment on it, even to get enthusiastic about it. They'd like their family members to do so as well. Even nicer would be if their friends would express an interest.

Early in my career, I was on a panel where the participants were asked about whether their family members read their work. Most said that they didn't. Several told stories filled with pathos about giving their latest work to a spouse or parent, only to have it put by unread. The audience was so sympathetic that more such tales were elicited.

I was actually embarrassed to admit that not only did my spouse read my stuff, so did my parents, most of my siblings, and even a few family members who had never read SF before trying mine.

When you think about it, this expectation that family members should take an interest in the writer's work is very egocentric. Does an accountant come home and expect everyone to go over that astonishingly complex incorporation agreement he wrote that day? Jim writes long, scholarly archeological reports. I read some parts. I read the articles he writes for a more "popular" audience, but he certainly doesn't expect me to follow all his work.

Why then should I expect him to follow mine?

Wanderings on Writing

I don't. I'm lucky that Jim was an SF/F reader long before we met and that he happens to take an interest in my writing. I'm lucky that he is also a great first reader and editor. But that's the point – I'm lucky. I know I'm lucky.

Being a writer does not make you the center of the universe.

Two: I'm a writer. Leave me alone.

I touched on this last week from the writer's perspective. However, when you think about it, this is an insanely selfish point of view. Yes, to write you need some time and space, but what do you give in return? Many writers expect to be given their space, but don't give much back.

My feeling is that, if you expect to be left alone to write, then you need to give time in return. In my case, I try to write when Jim is also working. Occasionally, he comes home to find the house dark and cold and me in the office pounding away on the keyboard. I look up and say, "The Muse hit at 5:30, sorry! Just a sec..." However, I don't make a habit of this. I made an adult choice to get married. I think I owe my marriage at least as much attention as my job.

Maybe the fact that I was "widowed" relatively young (Roger died when I was 32) gave me this un-American perspective toward my writing. Maybe I'm just an advocate of balance.

As I said in the previous piece, there is no single set of rules for how to live with a writer. I'll stress here that my solution is not everyone's solution. I know one night-owl writer who goes out of his way to make sure he's awake and up to have dinner with his family before going to write. I know another where the writer (who also has a fulltime job as a mom) makes sure her writing time is when her kid is otherwise occupied.

The point is, if a writer wants a healthy relationship, then part of the responsibility is on the writer – not solely on everyone else.

Jane Lindskold

Three: The Other Side of Staring at the Wall.

Last week I mentioned how writers can be working very hard indeed at those times when they don't appear to be working at all. I'm not saying this is incorrect, but I am saying that the rest of the family deserves some indication of when the writer is brainstorming and when the writer is just taking it easy.

I'll tell Jim, "I'm a bit stuck. I'm going to go make tonight's salad and see what comes loose." Then he's not completely surprised when he wanders in, and I wave the paring knife at him and say, "No! Don't talk to me! I'm writing."

Or I'll tell him, "I'm done for the day. I'm going off to…"

I think it's only polite to supply some indication of what you're doing. Otherwise, can your partner (or kids or parents or whatever) be blamed for thinking you're just goofing off?

Four: Don't Expect Them to Read Your Mind…

I mentioned last time how writers need a certain amount of stroking. Jim and I have been together long enough that he knows my creative pulse points pretty well. This wasn't always the case. I needed to explain to him why the arrival of – say – the cover art for a new book wasn't automatically a cause for jumping up and down. Instead, I might want his thoughtful assessment of whether he thought it was good or bad or suitable.

Give a hint of what you're looking for. "What do you think of this cover?" rather than "My new cover came today." Or say "I've just been reviewed in *PW*, I'm happy about that, but what do you think of…"

I put these statements down as I would make them. Only after did I see the interesting psychological revelation. "My new cover" not "My *book's* new cover." "I've just been reviewed…" not

Wanderings on Writing

"My *book* has just been reviewed." Writers do get too tangled up in identifying with our projects.

Anyhow, if you're precise about specifying what you'd like feedback on, both you and your family will be a lot happier. You, because you'll get the feedback you crave. Your associates, because they'll be able to avoid guessing what you're angling for and be helpful.

Five: Remember – You're Sharing the Space

Perhaps because the wild and crazy artists are the ones who get the press, some writers have the idea that being rude or inconsiderate is part of the turf, even what is needed to be a "real" writer. I don't believe it. If wearing a little black beret puts you in your "artistic" mind set, by all means, wear the beret (or sweater or whatever), but don't go raging all over the place, shouting about how you can't write without it...

Yeah, such eccentricities sound pretty dramatic – that is until you substitute "account" or "data process" for "write." Then it just sounds weird or self-indulgent.

Equally, if you need to play loud music to cut out the world, make sure the rest of the family can deal with it. If not, consider alternatives: closed doors, headphones, soundproofing. Or if you can't stand the background noise your family creates, consider ear plugs.

You might even need a separate office or to go to the library. Moreover, if you can't find a compromise, consider why. It could be an indication of uneven expectations on one side or the other. It might even indicate that you're trying to find excuses not to write and hoping to shift the blame to too much noise or too many distractions. Be honest with yourself and look for a solution, not a target.

Jane Lindskold

So... There are a few thoughts on how a writer can be a part of a vital relationship – or relationships – and still be creative. I hope they help!

What's a New Writer to Do?

More often than you might imagine, I get e-mails from unpublished novelists asking me for advice about the publishing business. I will admit, I take these queries most seriously when the person writing me has a project that is completed or nearly completed. Worrying about where to get an unwritten novel published just isn't practical. Even at the best of times, industry standards change. Lately, publishing seems to be changing on a monthly, if not weekly, basis.

Still, I'd like to help out if I can. When I was starting my own quest to get published, I was lucky to have a good friend – Roger Zelazny – who tutored me on the business. However, with hindsight, I realize I might have done better to also talk with someone who wasn't quite as established. Things had changed since Roger started out.... Although much of his advice was very good, some was distinctly dated.

So, here's what I'm going to do. I'm going to offer some advice meant to help those writers who have finished manuscripts in hand – manuscripts that are as polished and as perfect as their writers can make them.

Q: What's an advance? How much can I expect to get for my novel?

Wanderings on Writing

A: "Advance" is short for "advance against royalties." This is what a publisher pays you for the right to publish your book. The money is yours, free and clear. However, you don't get any additional money until the book has earned enough for the publisher to make back what they have advanced you. Royalties are based on a percentage of the cover price of the novel. Since these percentages vary from publisher to publisher, I won't go into that.

Brace yourself... The basic beginner's advance has not changed much in years. Usually, it is under $5,000.00, often much less. This is usually paid out in at least three segments: on-signing of the contract; on delivery and acceptance of the manuscript (this means the *revised* manuscript – after the editor has given you notes and you have addressed them in a satisfactory fashion); and on publication of the manuscript. Publishers are notorious for not being prompt in making these payments. You might sign the contract in April and not see the "on-signing" check until June.

The reason those million dollar advances make news is that they are rare occurrences.

Q: *Should I try for one of the big publishers or would a small "boutique" publisher be better for me?*

A: It depends on what you want. A big publisher will have a larger distribution network. That means they can get your books into all the chain stores. They have sales reps out there, telling all the independent booksellers about your book. They have a staff of editors, copy editors, art directors, and publicists in place. However, you won't be your editor's only concern. She (my last three editors have been female) will be working with other authors and other books at the same time as she is working with yours.

If you sell to a smaller publisher, you might get more personalized attention. On the other hand, that's not automatic. If this smaller publisher doesn't have a large staff, then your editor might be as overworked as at a larger publisher. Try to learn what sort of attention you can expect before signing with a smaller publisher. Also, try to find out what sort of distribution and promotional network they have in place.

Always be careful of "publishers" who want you to pay them to publish you...

Q: Do I even need a publisher?

A: That's a huge and controversial question. My answer would be that whether or not you need a publisher depends on the type of person you are. If you like self-promotion, enjoy spending lots of time on everything from formatting your own manuscript for publication, to art design, to promoting the work (a job that takes a lot of time), then self-publishing may be a good route for you.

If you can't do any one of those jobs, then you're going to need to pay someone to do it for you.

Although I've brought back into print some of my out-of-print works, I'm far from an expert on this area. It's also probably the fastest-evolving part of publishing so No One, no matter what anyone tells you, is an expert. If you're considering the self-publishing route, make sure you get many opinions.

Also, make sure that at least some of your opinions are from writers who do not already have a publication record or following. Seriously... It's easier to succeed in self-publishing if people already read your works. Many of the articles I've read raving about self-publishing as the next wave of the future have been written by writers who already have long track records. A couple of them have been major award winners. Last year I was on a panel with a fellow who has done very well in self-publishing. However, he had a following from his work in comics. Either way, he might have been proudly showing us his first published novel – but it was far from his first publication (and he was the first to admit it).

Q: I'm beginning to feel overwhelmed! Where do I look for current information on publishing?

A: If you want current, you want to look on the web. However, make sure you're getting a balanced presentation. There are lots of people who have strong opinions one way or another about everything. However, writers (because writing is what they do) are more likely to write these opinions down and put them where other people can find them. This doesn't mean that they're right.

Consider looking into professional writer's organizations. Joining a professional organization can be beneficial. These organizations will often have places on their websites where members can learn about publishers and new trends in publishing. There are organizations for many different genres – Science Fiction and Fantasy, Westerns, Horror, Romance, Mystery. Consider joining more than one for wider exposure to opinions.

Yes. You can join, even if you're not yet published. Look for information on "associate" memberships.

Many areas have regional writers' groups. I'm most familiar with Southwest Writers, here in New Mexico. These groups can be great for beginners. There are usually monthly meetings with guest speakers – usually published professionals. Frequently, the organization sponsors an annual conference or contest, both interesting ways to learn more about the business or to find out how your work measures up.

If you're interested in Science Fiction, Fantasy, or Horror, don't overlook your local SF convention. Often there is a track of writing-related programming that most expensive writers' conferences would envy.

Finally, come to your research on publishing with an open mind. A few years ago, I was on a panel at an academic writer's conference. One of the audience members asked about self-publishing. He clearly did not like the answers he received. Afterwards, I heard him ranting to someone in the corridor. Turns out he had self-published. He had expected to hear he was on the fast and easy road to big bucks and mega-success. Hearing that he was going to have to work hard had not sat well with him. In his opinion, the panel of five published authors were all idiots...

In other words, you can only learn how to succeed in publishing if you're willing to listen, to weigh advice, and to formulate a plan that works to your goals and to your strengths.

Learning to Write to Live

In "What's a New Writer to Do?", I wrote about things a new writer – in this case defined as someone who has a novel finished or nearly finished and was wondering about what to do next – might want to know.

When this piece appeared as part of my Wednesday Wanderings, the following query came in via e-mail: "I really liked what you wrote but, what is your advice for someone who is serious about writing professionally, but doesn't know quite where to start? Should I take courses on writing? How about workshops?"

Q: What is your advice for someone who is serious about writing professionally, but doesn't quite know where to start?

Wanderings on Writing

A: First make sure you really like to write – not just like the idea of having written. It's much easier to talk about your great story idea than it is to actually get the idea down on the page.

Next, consider what you're going to do to make a living until you start making enough money to give up your "day job." I strongly recommend not taking up a profession that involves a lot of writing – even if writing is what you're best at.

My experience – and I've heard this from other writers as well – is that each person has only a certain amount of writing in them on any given day. If you use that all up in your day job, then you're not going to have it when you come home in the evening and want to work on your novel. Even the difference between writing non-fiction and fiction is sometimes not enough to stop your brain and creativity from drying up.

Q: Should I take courses on writing?

A: Certainly you should take courses if you wish. Just don't major in creative writing!

Alternately, if you already have a career path, don't fool yourself into believing that taking courses on creative writing will suddenly make you publishable. In my experience, the only thing that numerous courses on creative writing – especially the type taught at most colleges – are good for is to give you the credentials to teach other people about creative writing.

Yes. A course or two can be useful, if for no other reason than that, if you take them seriously, they're going to teach you about writing to a deadline (always useful for a professional) and how to structure your day so that you make time to write. However, writing – a lot of writing – is what you need to do to refine your skills so that you can become a "pro."

Q: What about workshops?

Jane Lindskold

A: Workshops can be very useful. Many workshops address "genre" or "popular" fiction – a topic that is, sadly, anathema in many college courses. Therefore, if you're interested in writing Mysteries or Romance or Science Fiction or Fantasy or Thrillers or any other of the many forms of popular fiction, writing workshops may be of greater use to you than college courses.

There are workshops focused on specific genres. However, even workshops that aren't as tightly focused will offer lectures on subjects such as narrative hooks, researching, characterization, and keeping the plot moving – all of which you can apply to your own writing.

Writing workshops also often include lectures on the business side of writing. This can be very valuable, even if all you learn at first is the vocabulary of the trade. (You'd be amazed at how many would-be writers I've met who don't know the difference between a publisher and an editor, an agent and a publicist.) Especially during the more intensive workshops, you will have the opportunity to network, thereby making contacts with writers and other professionals that may be valuable for years to come.

Since writers' workshops can be expensive, both in time (some run several weeks) and in money, research your potential options before signing up. Take a look at the schedule before attending and map out those lectures you want to attend.

Some workshops offer an opportunity for attendees to sign up for a short interview with an agent or editor. I wouldn't recommend attending a workshop in the hopes that this will be your big break. However, such pitch sessions are something you'll rarely find as part of a college course.

Q: If I shouldn't major – or take lots of courses – about writing, then what should I do to prepare myself to be a professional writer?

A: First, train for a day job that you'll either like or that at least won't drain away your creative energy while you work on your writing. Even better, consider a job that will stimulate your creativity. Just among New Mexico writers, I know an environmental engineer, a physicist, several lawyers, a couple journalists, myriad computer geeks, a doctor, and a couple of teachers. All of them have, at one time or another, drawn on their professions in their fiction..

Second, consider taking a course or two on subjects like contracts and accounting. Yes. I'm serious.

From the minute you sell your first story – even a short story for half-a-cent a word – you're going to be signing contracts. At the beginning of their careers, many writers don't have an agent to advise them on what to sign and what not to sign, so it's a good idea to be familiar with the basic form of contracts. Did you know you're not required to accept everything in a contract? However, knowing what is negotiable and what is non-negotiable will be a matter of learning your profession.

Why take courses in accounting? First, you're going to need to declare any income you make from writing. That means no more EZ tax forms. If you're going to itemize your deductions, you'll need to file various additional forms. It also helps to know what you can deduct and under what circumstances. Yes. You can pay an accountant to prepare your tax forms. (I do.) However, you're still required to supply the accountant with the basic information. Since most accountants charge based upon the time they need to do the job, the better prepared you are in advance, the more money you'll save.

Many people think the life of a writer is filled with creativity and imagination. It is. However, if you want to sell what you write, you need to accept that writing is also a business and educate yourself accordingly. I've known a couple of writers who didn't bother to do so and they're paying for their ignorance, either in lost rights or in cold, hard, cash.

Q: That's a lot to think about. Anything else?

A: Yes. Although courses and workshops may help you, the only way to become a professional writer is to write, to submit what you write, and to keep doing so until you finally "make it." (See the previous essay you want my views on self-publishing.)

Recognize that writing as a career – rather than as an art or hobby – involves more than knowing how to tell a good tale. I promise, you won't regret it!

Writing: The Art and Craft

There is a complex, intertwined relationship between what I think of as the art of writing and the craft of writing.

The art of writing involves rich characterization, thoughtful world-building, and intricate but comprehensible plots. "Art" also involves the elusive but all important element of style – that strange but often undefinable element that means you'll never mistake a Terry Pratchett novel for a Patricia McKillip novel, even if these authors were to write on the same subject, about the same characters, and in the same setting.

The craft of writing is what it takes to write and write well. This starts with actually sitting down to write, rather than talking about that great novel you could write if you only had time. It carries through to keeping writing day after day, until the pages pile up. It continues as you revise what you've written, trying to make the words bring the vision you started with into a shape that you can share it with someone else.

Wanderings on Writing

Obviously, the two are intertwined. You can't improve in the art of writing if you don't actually sit down and write. Writing workshops or books on writing can teach you tricks and terminology but, just as you can't learn to ride a horse without throwing your leg over the back of that big, hairy four-legged beastie, you can't learn to write unless you put words down on a page (or screen). And not just a few words, but lots and lots. There's an old saying that it takes three falls to make a rider. I'll adapt that and say that it takes three hundred thousand words to make a writer.

However, you can't produce writing that is worth reading if you don't attend to the art. Otherwise, you're always going to collect rejection letters or, if you choose to self-publish, never get that vital "buzz" that leads to people insisting that their friends absolutely *must* read your book.

Sometimes, art and craft become very out of balance. I've known art-obsessed writers who worry so much about making sure that every detail and word is perfect that they don't write very much. Of course, what they write is often beautiful. Ultimately, their slim, slowly-evolving manuscripts can become like one of those haute cuisine meals that are appealing to look at, delightful to taste, and not very filling. They leave you wanting more, but the "more" isn't there.

On the other hand, I've known writers – including many popular professionals – who become so caught up in producing to a deadline that art falls by the wayside. The same wonderful word-slinging skills that brought them to where they are professionally fall to the wayside, becoming less important than producing "copy." Art vanishes. Taking its place is a strange race to finish a work and get it "out. " In the end, production goals become more important than the dreams and visions that led the person to take up writing.

Some people say there is no difference between the art and craft of writing. Maybe so. I prefer to see them as two sides of a balance scale. Sometimes one will over-balance the other, but to achieve the best results, the two sides should be kept about level.

Acknowledgments

I'd like to thank all the people who helped to make this book possible.

Emily Mah Tippetts was wonderful transforming the manuscript into both an e-book and a POD. I highly recommend the services of her company, E.M. Tippetts Book Designs (http://www.em-tippettsbookdesigns.com). Working with on her on cover design was loads of fun! I can't wait to do it again.

Tori Hansen painted the original watercolor that became the cover. I had a marvelous time watching how a piece of art comes to life, from line drawing to final painting. And I'll always treasure watching Tori working in the middle of my living room floor, gently shoving away cats who clearly thought they should be painting, too.

Jim Moore, Paul Dellinger, and Yvonne Coats all helped with proofing a manuscript in which I was absolutely certain I'd caught every potential problem – and hadn't. Doubtless we missed something, but it wasn't for lack of trying.

Finally, I want to thank all the readers of my Wednesday Wanderings blog for encouraging me to write about writing. It's been fun!

Other books by Jane Lindskold

Artemis Awakening Series
Artemis Awakening
Artemis Invaded (coming June, 2015)

The Firekeeper Series
Through Wolf's Eyes
Wolf's Head, Wolf's Heart
The Dragon of Despair
Wolf Captured
Wolf Hunting
Wolf's Blood

The Breaking the Wall Series
Thirteen Orphans
Nine Gates
Five Odd Honors

The Buried Pyramid

Child of a Rainless Year

The Athanor Series
Changer
Changer's Daughter (aka *Legends Walking*)

Brother to Dragons, Companion to Owls

Marks of Our Brothers

Pipes of Orpheus

Chronomaster

Smoke and Mirrors

When the Gods are Silent

With Roger Zelazny

Donnerjack

Lord Demon

With David Weber

Fire Season

Treecat Wars

44489626R00113

Made in the USA
Charleston, SC
28 July 2015